READY FOR

By the same author:
Trumpet Call to Prayer

Ready for His Return?

Alerting God's People to the Signs of the Times

RAYMOND BORLASE

THANKFUL BOOKS

Copyright © Raymond Borlase 2007

First published 2007

Published by Thankful Books
c/o P.O. Box 2118, Seaford BN25 9AR.
in association with Intercessors For Britain
8 Eastfields Road, School Aycliffe,
County Durham, DL5 6QH

ISBN 978 1 905084 13 5

Unless otherwise indicated, biblical quotations are
from the New American Standard Bible © The Lockman
Foundation 1960, 1962, 1963, 1968, 1971, 1972, 1973.

Book design and production for the publisher by
Bookprint Creative Services, <www.bookprint.co.uk>
Printed in Great Britain.

CONTENTS

FOREWORD

In writing this book, I have been very conscious that I am often treading on dangerous ground. I recognise that I am opening myself to all sorts of attacks from believers who hold diverse views on the Second Coming. Obviously, I do come from a certain persuasion on these matters. I have never sought to follow some doctrinal position delineated by others, and I have always tried to avoid being too dogmatic on the position I hold. I am very much aware that many of the Jews had such a fixed position regarding the Messiah that when He came, they did not recognise Him.

My views come from having read through the Scriptures over sixty times now. I say that, not to boast, but to show that I prefer to study the Scriptures rather than theologians. I would encourage you to do the same. Study and meditate on the Scriptures for yourself and search these things out.

This is, therefore, not a definitive doctrine on the Second Coming. I would prefer to leave that to others. The purpose

of this book is to call Christians to be ready for the days that
lead up to His return. In doing so, I inevitably will have to
challenge the views of many within the Church. I do not do so
for the sake of controversy, but for the sake of being prepared.
I would urge, therefore, that where we disagree on interpretation, you will not come with a closed mind to what I am
writing. I may be wrong on certain points, or you may have a
clearer understanding than I have on certain aspects of the
Lord's return, but I believe that God has called me to write this
book so that you may be *ready for His return*. I believe much
of the Church is ill-prepared for the days which lie ahead.

Above all, I do not want to produce some intellectual elite
who are absolutely correct on all points of doctrine, but to
warn believers of what we need to expect in the last days and
to be earnestly looking for His appearing, Whom we love and
serve.

In interpreting the Scriptures, I believe that the principles
which were laid down by the Reformers are basically right.
First of all, the straightforward reading of scripture is to be the
accepted understanding. Once we try to manipulate the text
to fit our interpretation, then we are mishandling the Word.
Secondly, any verse needs to be examined in the light of
its immediate context. So many have misinterpreted Scripture
because they ignore the surrounding passage thus distorting
the meaning of the verse. Thirdly, Scripture needs to be compared with Scripture to give a complete view. One Scripture
which appears to contradict another needs to be weighed one
against the other and the apparent contradiction resolved.
You cannot ignore the verse which seems to contradict your
own position. In other words, every verse needs to be balanced

against the whole context of Scripture. Finally, as Peter reminds us, the interpretation of Scripture is not left to the individual. The Holy Spirit inspired the Word, it is the Holy Spirit who reveals the truth (2 Peter 1:20, 21). We need to prayerfully seek a right understanding. These are principles I have sought to employ in considering the subject of the Lord's Return.

January 2007

CHAPTER ONE

THE SIGNS OF THE TIMES

Many Bible-believing Christians accept that we are very much in the last days. Of course, to be biblically correct, the last days run between the first coming of Jesus and His return, but as world events increasingly unfold, we see just how near the return of the Lord is.

Jesus gave various signs regarding His return, including wars, rumours of wars, famines and earthquakes. He said that these were merely the beginning of birth pains (see Matthew 24:6–8). One thing about birth pains is that they become more intense and frequent towards the point of birth. The world has been plunged into two awful world wars during the twentieth century that still leave many people scarred by those conflicts. Africa has seen some of the most appalling atrocities, to say nothing about Muslim militants attacking the twin towers of New York's World Trade Center. While there have always been famines, the scale of disaster is immense because of the increased world population. A famine in biblical times was a disaster, but the deaths would be numbered in thousands, whereas today they are numbered in millions. The same is true of earthquakes.

We are constantly hearing of global warming and 2004 and 2005 were seen to be the worst hurricane seasons for many decades. Whether it is a result of man's activity or God's judgement upon a wicked world can be endlessly debated, but one thing is clear: Jesus said the end-times would be marked by "dismay among nations, in perplexity at the roaring of the sea and the waves, men fainting from fear and the expectation of the things which are coming upon the world . . ." He adds, "Then they will see the Son of Man coming in a cloud with power and great glory" (Luke 21:25–27).

The reference to "the roaring of the sea and the waves" has added significance when we remember the earthquake which took place just off the coast of Sumatra on Boxing Day, 2004. It registered nine on the Richter Scale; one of the most powerful on Earth. (Exactly a year before, on Boxing Day, there was also an earthquake in Bam, Iran. Was that a coincidence? I think not. Perhaps we should note that both are Muslim countries.) That earthquake of 2004 unleashed a tsunami (tidal wave) that travelled at 300 miles per hour, and in places ranged from thirty to over a hundred feet high. It devastated coastal regions in Indonesia, Thailand, Burma, India, Sri Lanka and even across to Somalia and Kenya. Various islands were swamped, including the Maldives, the Andaman and Nicobar Islands. At least 250,000 were swept to their deaths as a result of the earthquake and the resulting tsunami. It was the worst natural disaster in living memory.

As the tsunami swept in from the sea, there was a terrifying roar with the waves' advance towards the shore. I had previously always thought of the reference to "the roaring of the seas" in terms of waves being whipped up by hurricane force winds pounding the beach, but I now understand that the prophetic words of Jesus could equally refer to a tsunami. The mention, too, of men's hearts failing them for fear at the things coming upon the earth could quite literally mean that some would die of a heart attack, as some did as a result of that tsunami. Whether we consider the hurricanes of Florida, or the tsunami sweeping across the Indian Ocean, 2004 was a terrifying time as far as "the roaring of the seas and the waves" were concerned.

It is perhaps worthy of note that the epicentre of the earthquake was just off the Banda Aceh province of Indonesia. That area has been one where Christians have been brutally persecuted by Muslims. Indeed, so many of those countries affected by the tsunami have persecuted Christians and opposed the gospel, yet Christians were able to take aid into those desperate regions. It was interesting that it was the West which gave most aid while the oil-rich Muslim countries did little to help their fellow Muslims.

In Thailand, the Buddhists did little to help, but Christians again gave aid. Along the coastal strip most affected in Thailand, twenty churches were established within twelve months of the tsunami striking.

The events of Boxing Day, 2004, were followed up by one of the worst hurricanes ever experienced in America. Hurricane Katrina, as it was named, was a category five hurricane, the highest designated category. While it devastated much of the property in the surrounding area, it was New Orleans which experienced the greatest damage. Thirty-foot waves pounded the coastline, but it was the breaching of the levees which caused the real damage. These dykes protected the city which is mainly below sea level. The hurricane hit New Orleans on Monday, 29th August 2005. The next day the levees were breached and the city was flooded. The timing could not have been more significant as an act of God. New Orleans had been preparing not originally for a hurricane, but for its Southern Decadence annual homosexual celebration. It was due on 31st August, the day after the city was flooded.

Repent America, an evangelical Christian organisation, reported that "Southern Decadence has a history of filling the French Quarter section of the city with drunken homosexuals engaging in sex acts in the public streets and bars." The previous year "a local pastor sent video footage of sex acts being performed in front of police to the mayor, city council, and the media. City officials simply ignored the footage and continued to welcome and praise the weeklong celebration as being an 'exciting event'." It was expected that 150,000 revellers would have gathered for the event.

"New Orleans is also known for its Mardi Gras parties where thousands of drunken men revel in the streets to exchange plastic jewellery for drunken women to expose their breasts" (Repent America). Peter Sheridan of the *Daily Express* also referred to this as "an annual bacchanalia of drunken debauchery and hedonistic over indulgence each February." He spoke of the city as being not only the home of jazz, but also that "voodoo stalked its darkest corners, a terrifying blend of religion and witchcraft brought across by African slaves."

As Sky Television reported on the aftermath of Hurricane Katrina, one woman who was a resident of New Orleans said, "the Good Lord has judged New Orleans." I cannot disagree with her view. The timing was no coincidence. The city authorities had ignored the previous warning from the pastor to its detriment.

During Ramadan of 2005, Pakistan experienced its worse natural disaster when it was struck by an earthquake of 7.6 on the Richter Scale. Over 73,000 people died in that disaster, yet Muslims believe that Ramadan is a time when they are particularly safe. Once again, we see another Islamic nation convulsed by natural disasters.

I have no doubt that the very events that Jesus prophesied concerning earthquakes and the roaring of the waves are being fulfilled in these various catastrophes which we are experiencing in our days. They are not simply accidents of nature, but God expressing His divine displeasure against nations which are becoming increasingly wicked and rebellious.

I cannot leave this matter without referring to Hebrews 12:26f. The writer of that letter quoted from Haggai 2:6 by saying, "Yet once more I will shake not only the earth, but also the Heaven." The Greek word which is used for "shake" is *seio*; its future is *seiso*, and the noun derived from it is *seismos* (meaning earthquake), from which we get our word seismic. It is plain from this that God is literally going to shake the earth, hence Jesus' reference to earthquakes as a sign of His return and the "birth" of God's new order – the reign of Jesus on earth!

Jesus warned, too, not only of earthquakes and signs in sun, moon and stars, but that "the powers that are in the heavens will be shaken" (Mark 13:25). The word for "shake" here is *saleuo* which means "to shake or agitate". Those powers refer to what Paul calls, in Ephesians 6, "principalities and powers . . . in the heavenly places." Isaiah 24 speaks of the earth being shaken violently and tottering, but also that "the Lord will punish the host of heaven on high" (v. 21).

We understand from Scripture that demonic powers seek to dominate our world and turn people from the one true God and His Son Jesus Christ. But a day of reckoning is coming for Satan and his forces. With the return of Christ, antichrist will be destroyed and Satan will be banished. No wonder they quake!

Referring back again to Hebrews 12, the writer states that God's voice shook (*saleuo*) the earth at Sinai (vv. 18f, 26), but now He would literally shake the earth (*seio*), so what could not be shaken (or agitated, *saleuo*) would remain; namely His unshakeable Kingdom.

The passage really is a call to Christians to get their priorities right. When everything is shaking around us, let us make sure that we focus on God's Kingdom and consequently "offer to God an acceptable service with reverence and awe" (v. 28). The signs which we have witnessed are the increasing "birth pains" which will herald the return of the Lord Jesus Christ, and His Kingdom on earth.

However, I do believe there is a significance in this passage regarding the unbeliever. You may remember that there was an earthquake when Paul was in jail at Philippi. A very frightened jailer thinking he might be killed by the prisoners, now at large as a result of the earthquake, asked: "Sirs, what must I do to be saved?" Paul's response was immediate: "Believe in the Lord Jesus, and you shall be saved, you and your whole household" (Acts 16:31). They believed and were baptised. As a result of the shaking (the earthquake), they were brought into the unshakeable Kingdom.

We have heard of backsliders who returned to the Lord, and others who were saved as a result of the tsunami. Also a number of churches were also established in many of the areas affected.

The Billy Graham Association reported, a few months after Katrina struck, that the city was more open to God. They wrote that "since Katrina, pastors have seen people turning to prayer as never before." The pastor of First Baptist Church said, "This continuing tragedy has brought our city to its knees". Another leader said, "After the worst natural disaster in the history of this nation, never has this area been more open to spiritual renewal" (*Decision*, March/April 2006).

We might bear in mind, too, the words of the prophet Joel, quoted by Peter in Acts 2:20, 21: "The sun shall be turned into darkness, and the moon into blood, before the great and awesome day of the Lord shall come. And it shall be, that everyone who calls on the name of the Lord shall be saved." In the midst of the shaking, there is still time to be saved prior to the return of the Lord. Once Jesus has returned, the day of salvation will have drawn to a close – the day of judgement will have been ushered in.

There were other indications which Jesus gave concerning His return. He said that the conditions at that time would be just like in the days of Noah and Lot. We shall consider this in the next chapter but, for many of us, as we observe the moral standards of the nation and of the international community, we can see the similarity.

Jesus also warned of false prophets and messiahs, false signs and wonders with increasing deception which would lead to many of God's people being deceived. Again, many of us have observed in the western world the increase of the number of false teachings which abound in the Church. The Word of Faith and the prosperity gospel messages have affected the Church worldwide together with the effect of the so-called Toronto blessing. False messianic movements have been seen in Africa and even in Jewish circles. The desire for somebody to solve the world's problems, including terrorism, will leave the world prone to following any messianic figure who promises peace.

On the more positive side, although Jesus warned of false prophets and increased lawlessness, with a falling away among believers, He stated that "This gospel of the kingdom shall be preached in the whole world as a testimony to all the nations, and then the end will come" (Matthew 24:14). There is no doubt that it is our generation which has seen the global impact of the gospel. Since the ministries of Whitefield and the Wesley brothers in America and Britain, during the eighteenth century, we have seen what has become known as the modern missionary movement. William Carey was one of the first men who tried to demonstrate to a complacent church that the other nations needed to hear the gospel and eventually went to India. Men like David Livingstone went to Africa and Hudson Taylor to China. Continents were opening up to the good news concerning Jesus. Wycliffe Translators began to produce the Scriptures in hundreds of languages.

In the days of the apostles, the gospel quickly spread to the whole of the Mediterranean countries, and on into India, Egypt and Ethiopia, but the last 250 years have seen a new burst of missionary zeal with the gospel going to the far-flung corners of the world. Modern technology and broadcasting have meant that even where missionaries cannot enter, the good news concerning Jesus has winged its way on the airwaves. Even Saudi Arabia cannot stop the gospel entering its territory, whether by gospel broadcasts or through Bibles which were smuggled in during the first Gulf war.

Some make the mistake that the whole world will be christianised, but Jesus simply said the gospel would be preached in the whole world as a witness or testimony. He never stated that the whole world would be saved; in fact, He warned that there would be few who would find the narrow way leading to life. However, this sign, that the gospel would be preached "in the whole world" is being fulfilled in our day.

There is another sign that not all Christians will accept. It amazes me that this is the case, but they seem to think that the modern state of Israel is an accident of history. I notice that the apostle Paul states that God "made from one man every nation of mankind to live on all the face of the earth, having determined their appointed times and the boundaries of their habitation" (Acts 17:26). God determines the times and boundaries of the nations. On that basis alone, Israel cannot be an accident of history. The fact that it came into being after 2,000 years of exile for the Jews, and that it has survived so many wars since it was established is, in itself, a witness to God's purpose.

We have to bear in mind also that Jesus was asked, after His resurrection, "Lord, is it at this time You are restoring the kingdom to Israel?" His reply was simply this. "It is not for you to know times or epochs which the Father has fixed by His own authority . . ." (Acts 1:6, 7). Their responsibility was to proclaim the gospel and they would receive the Holy Spirit to enable them in that task. Jesus, however, never denied their presumption that sovereignty would be restored to Israel. How could He when He had told them already that it would be restored?

How did He do that? Well, take the lesson of the fig tree. He stated that when the fig tree "puts forth its leaves, you will know summer is near. Even so, you too, when you see these things happening, recognise that He [Jesus, on His return] is near, right at the door" (Mark 13:28, 29). Why did Jesus not simply say when the leaves on the trees appear, but refer specifically to the fig tree? Why be so particular?

The fig tree was often used to refer to Israel. For instance, in Hosea 9:10, God says: "I found Israel like grapes in the wilderness; I saw your fathers as the earliest fruit on the fig tree in its first season." It is all the more interesting that Jesus tells a parable of a man who had a fig tree. For three years the owner of the vineyard had come looking for fruit on the fig tree. As it had not borne any fruit he told the vineyard-keeper to cut it down. The gardener suggested it should be root-pruned and given some fertiliser and a further period of time. The significant thing is that the period of three years is mentioned. Jesus' ministry lasted just three years! What fruit was Jesus looking for? Repentance! The context in which Jesus gave this parable was concerning two disasters which had happened in Israel. In referring to those disasters, Jesus asked the question as to whether they considered that those who had been killed were greater sinners than the rest living in Israel, and twice he added this statement: "I tell you, no, but unless you repent, you will likewise perish" (See Luke 13:1–9). He was calling them to repent. He had begun His ministry just as John the Baptist had by saying, "Repent for the Kingdom of Heaven is at hand" (Matthew 4:17).

It is also interesting that Jesus cursed the fig tree in Mark 11:12–14. He had come looking to see if there were figs on it, but there was "nothing but leaves, for it was not the season for figs." How unfair of Jesus to curse it when it was not the right time for figs! Surely, there must be some significance in His actions. What we have here is a dramatic parable being played out. He had previously spoken of the fig tree not bearing fruit (repentance): now He is dramatically showing that Israel will wither and die (as was previously stated in the parable – "You will likewise perish"). There will be a season when Israel will come to repentance and faith in Jesus as Messiah, Saviour and Lord as Paul shows in Romans 11:25, 26, but this was the "season" when they would reject the call to repentance and reject Jesus as Saviour. This would lead to their destruction as a nation, just as Jesus prophesied on other occasions. The fig tree would wither and die.

Mark records that the next morning, as the disciples were passing the fig tree, they notice that it had "withered from the roots up" (11:20). If we follow through Mark's record, it is that same afternoon when Jesus prophesied concerning the temple that "not one stone will be left upon another which will not be torn down" (Mark 13:2). That literally happened in AD 70 when Jerusalem was destroyed. The fig tree had died! Jesus, however, continued to talk about the events leading up to His return. He states that when the fig tree puts forth its leaves, it is a sure sign that summer is coming and His return is near.

In using that illustration of the fig tree sprouting, the significance would not be lost on them. Just the day before, they had seen Jesus' action in cursing the fig tree. That very morning they had seen it dead! They had previously heard the parable of the owner of the fig tree who had looked for fruit for three years. They had heard the warning that if they did not repent, they would likewise perish. Then within hours, Jesus is talking, not simply of the destruction of the temple, but that prior to His return the fig tree would put forth its leaves. If the withering of the fig tree was speaking of Israel's demise, then surely the reference to it putting forth leaves must speak of the "resurrection" of Israel as a nation.

Interestingly, Luke's gospel records Jesus as saying that "all the trees" would put forth their leaves as well as the fig tree (Luke 21:29). Israel came to birth as a nation in 1948 with many other nations gaining their independence and sovereignty about that time – India, Pakistan, and many African nations.

We should note, too, that prior to the reference to the fig tree and the other trees, Jesus stated that Jerusalem would be destroyed and the Jewish people scattered and "led captive into all the nations; and Jerusalem will be trampled under foot by the Gentiles until the times of the Gentiles are fulfilled (or completed)" (Luke 21:24). In 1967, Jerusalem came back under Jewish sovereignty.

Here, therefore, are two significant signs concerning the time of Christ's return: a sovereign Jewish state (1948), and Jerusalem once again under Jewish control (1967). Added to that, we see that in our generation the gospel, especially as a result of radio and TV, has been presented worldwide. The end is near!

CHAPTER TWO

THE END IS NEAR

> The end of all things is near; therefore, be of sound judgement and sober spirit for the purpose of prayer. (1 Peter 4:7)

I trust that the point has been made as to the end of all things and the return of Christ, but certain matters must follow from that. We have to be of "sound judgement and sober spirit".

Sound judgement is essential for the end-times. As we have already noted, one of the marks of the last days will be deception. If that is the case, then it is imperative that we carefully examine movements, ministries and their messages. We can only do that if we know what the Word of God teaches.

If we take the matter of movements, we need to be careful that we do not get carried away by the impact and popularity of any movement. The charismatic movement rightly emphasised the baptism of the Holy Spirit together with the gifts of the Spirit, and brought new life to the Church, but within its ranks there were some who were teaching error. It is easy to

24

be led astray by the excitement and emotion of what is happening without examining it carefully.

The Toronto blessing is a clear example of this. All sorts of things were attributed to the work of the Spirit, but it had no foundation in Scripture. Some were claiming to be struck dumb through the "anointing", but when Peter was filled with the Spirit, he spoke boldly. Some stated that they were drunk with the Spirit, but nowhere in Scripture do we see people displaying that sort of behaviour. They may have accused Peter and the disciples of being drunk because of their boldness. Was it a matter of "Dutch courage", as we say, or was it the power of the Holy Spirit that made them bold? Peter was certainly coherent and in control. Indeed, one of the marks of the Holy Spirit is self-control, so how come people could speak of "uncontrollable laughter" happening as a result of the Holy Spirit? Why did many produce animal noises when the work of the Spirit is to make us more like Jesus? Nebuchanezzar may have behaved like an animal, but it was not by the Spirit of God, but under the judgement of God.

In spite of these things and many other matters, people succumbed to the propaganda produced by its proponents. People were deceived. They were sadly lacking in sound judgement.

Ministries may claim to have an anointing, but it does not matter how great the following; they need to be carefully examined. They may produce all sorts of unusual phenomena, but that does not mean they are of God. There will be false prophets, false christs (literally "anointings") with false signs and wonders, but they are false! Watch out!

The message is so often the give-away. Again, one has to exercise sound judgement. Scripture can be quoted, but twisted. One such false teacher speaking about Toronto and inviting people to come forward to receive "the blessing" said that they should not think about it "for the natural mind cannot understand the things of God." Unfortunately, he did not add what appears later in the same passage: ". . . but we have the mind of Christ" (1 Corinthians 2:16). As believers we do not fall into the category of the "natural man" who lacks revelation about God and His ways, but He has revealed to us the things of God, by His Spirit. We should think, therefore, about these things, and indeed we should test the spirits to see if they are of God. This false teacher, under the guise of Scripture, had totally misled people into unthinking acceptance of what was happening. He also told people not to pray as they came forward, but simply receive. If prayer is a hindrance to receiving the so-called blessing, then there is something wrong! The alarm bells should have been ringing loud and clear, but many were deceived into acceptance.

The Bereans did not accept Paul's teaching at face value, but they examined the Scriptures to see if Paul's message was right. The writer to the Hebrews reminds us that "solid food" (the meatier parts of God's Word) "is for the mature, who because of practice have their senses trained to discern good and evil" (5:14). God's Word, as it is applied to various situations and circumstances, equips us to know what is right or wrong, what is of God, what is of the flesh, and what is of Satan. The trouble is that too many Christians are ignorant today of the Word of God, hence they lack sound judgement.

Peter tells us also that we should be of "sober spirit". The Greek word literally means that we should be free of intoxicants. This word is used six times in Scripture and it is always used in a metaphorical sense rather than literal. A person who is sober is able to weigh up a situation. The person who is drunk is often completely incapable of knowing what is happening around him or her. His or her mind is blurred; he may even see things that are not there; he does not have proper control of his faculties.

A believer needs to have his (or her) "wits about him", as we say, especially in the last days. Again and again, when Jesus was speaking about His return, He warned His followers to "be on the alert." It is not the time to be "sozzled", "switched off", or slumbering. In fact Paul uses such terminology in talking about the last days. He says that they should not be drunk or sleeping. He uses this same Greek word which Peter uses when he says, "let us be on the alert and sober . . ." Then he adds: "Since we are of the day, let us be sober . . ." He warns us that the day of the Lord could overtake us like a thief if we are not careful (see 1 Thessalonians 5:4–8 and Revelation 3:3). We need to be of sound judgement and sober spirit in the end-times.

Peter tells us, however, that the main reason for exercising good judgement and being alert is that we may pray. It is for the purpose of prayer! It seems to me that some Christians, realising that the return of Jesus is near, want to retreat into some mediaeval castle, pull up the drawbridge and sit it out in security and splendid isolation until the Lord returns. That is not the apostle's purpose; neither is it the purpose of God.

Jesus, in referring to His return, speaks of the faithful servant who takes care of his household "to give them their food at the proper time" (Matthew 24:42–44). Too many Christians have withdrawn into their hermitage instead of trying to feed their brothers and sisters and care for them. We all need to be ready to encourage and instruct other believers from the Scriptures. What I see, however, is that many Christians, because of deceptions, disappointments, and hurts, have withdrawn from the battle to nurse their wounds instead of pouring oil and wine into the wounds of others.

Equally, there is a danger that we, as Christians, see the wickedness of the world and its governments, and are aware of the spiritual battles which are taking place, but we sit clothed in our armour in some hiding place away from the conflict. I am not suggesting that we become some "militant tendency" of Christian politics or become Christian terrorists, but that we understand that our battle is still with principalities and powers. Sound judgement and a sober spirit are necessary that we might know how to pray in the right way.

Do not pray that the whole Church of God will be refined and that God will remove all apostate bishops, for God has told us that apostasy will be one of the marks of the age. Do not pray that the whole world will be converted or for some massive end-time revival. That is not the scenario which Scripture paints of the end-times. Again, we should not be supporting or praying for false prophets or teachers and their ministries. We might pray that some may be delivered from their error, but even then we need the witness in our spirits that they will turn.

We need to be aware of what God is doing. Right up to the end, God will be wanting to save people. We see from the book of Revelation that the Church (the Bride) will make herself ready with those righteous deeds. Therefore we should pray for the true Church to be refined.

We also see that antichrist will come before the return of the Lord, so we cannot pray against his appearance, but we can pray that God will bring about his final downfall and usher in the Kingdom of God.

As I read Scripture – both Old and New Testament – I see there is a point at which "all Israel is saved" when the hardness is taken away (Romans 11:26). Don't tell me that "Israel" there means the Church, as some say. Just prior to that it speaks of the fullness of the Gentiles having come in, in contrast to Israel. The whole chapter speaks about the rejection of the Jews and their stumbling over their Messiah. Yet through the Jews' rejection of Jesus, salvation has come to the Gentiles. Therefore if it is speaking of Israel's rejection as a nation, then Israel's salvation must mean the Jewish nation (not the Church). In any case, if the word "Israel" is interpreted there as the Church when Paul states that Israel will be saved, the meaning of the following verse (v. 28) becomes nonsensical! It means that the Church becomes the enemy of the gospel. Paul also continues by saying that they (Israel) are still beloved for the fathers sake (the Patriarchs) and that "the calling of God is irrevocable."

We have to watch world events concerning Israel, realising that God is seeking to bring them to Himself. Here we need sound, sober judgement not based on the media's perception, but on God's written Word. If Jesus confirms that God in His own time will restore the sovereignty of Israel – the fig tree putting forth its leaves, and Jerusalem coming under Jewish control again, leading to all Israel being saved – then this is a major item for prayer. Indeed Paul states that their rejection of Christ brought reconciliation for the world, and then states that their acceptance of Christ will bring "life from the dead" (Romans 11:15) which I believe will lead to the return of Christ and the resurrection of the dead with the Kingdom of God being ushered in.

Obviously Satan will do all that he can to hinder, if not prevent, the purposes of God. This is one of the reasons why most of the Muslim world is against Israel. It is not really the Palestinian issue; that is merely an excuse. Indeed the very Palestinian situation has come about because in 1967 Syria, Egypt and Jordan tried to drive out Israel; but in the end, Israel was victorious and conquered the territory often referred to as the West Bank and Gaza. Prior to that there was no peace for Israel, so the West Bank is not the real issue!

The Hadith (meaning tradition, and accepted alongside the Koran) states: "The Hour (of resurrection) will not take place until the Muslims fight the Jews, and kill them. And the Jews will hide behind the rock and tree, and the rock and tree will say: 'Oh Muslim, oh servant of Allah, this is a Jew behind me, come and kill him!' "

Again, we have to say if deception is going to be a major problem leading up to His return, as Jesus said it would be, then we have to watch and pray regarding these things. We need to understand matters very clearly, making sure we are not deceived, and to pray that many believers may be delivered from deception.

If there is going to be an apostate Church, then it may mean that there are sections of the so-called church for which we can no longer pray. Indeed, we may need to pray against certain sections of the Church, that God will negate their influence. We will need to pray against New Age influences and those of many other religions as they seek to lead people astray. There is only one name under heaven by which men shall be saved. Jesus is the only way to the Father. We dare not compromise on these issues.

Clearly, of course, we will need to pray for our fellow believers because many of them will face persecution. Yet we need to pray that even in the darkest days, the voice of truth will never be silent so that those who are lost may know the ways of God. We cannot follow the world's agenda and accept a man and woman living together without first being married. We cannot accept that homosexuality is right. If the Church is "the pillar and ground of truth" (1 Timothy 3:15), then we need to pray that the true Church of God will proclaim God's truth.

We see too, from the Word of God, that a world leader will emerge called the antichrist. We need to be aware of the political events which will surround his emergence, and pray that some may not be deceived by his activities. We may need to pray that "the people who know their God will display strength and take action" (Daniel 11:32). These words were probably written in the first place regarding the Jews who would resist the influence of Antiochus Epiphanes, an antichrist-type figure who came on the scene about 175–163 BC. Surely, however, it is an encouragement to us that God has the last word and that the antichrist will be overthrown at the return of Jesus.

These are just a few examples of what we are likely to face in the last days. Consequently, we need sound judgement and a sober spirit (being alert) to assess the situation correctly. It is no good relying on the world's media, for they do not understand the purposes of God: indeed, they are being motivated by Satan who blinds their eyes to spiritual realities. It is one reason why we need to read the Word of God regularly that we might understand His purposes, and how He works. Then we shall have a clearer understanding as to how we are to pray. Prayer will be absolutely vital in the final days, so we had better make a start now before the days become more difficult for believers.

CHAPTER THREE

THE DAYS OF LOT AND NOAH

Jesus was asked by the Pharisees "when the Kingdom of God was coming" (Luke 17:20). It would seem that they were looking for some specific event which would usher in the Kingdom, for He replied, "The Kingdom of God is not coming with signs to be observed; nor will they say, 'Look, here it is!' or, 'There it is!' " Then He added: "the Kingdom of God is in your midst (or, within you)."

Although we believe that the fullness of the Kingdom will be ushered in with the return of Christ – a unique event – for them the establishment of the Kingdom was different. It would not be in some spectacular event, but would be in the hearts and minds of His followers. Both John the Baptist and Jesus preached: "Repent, for the Kingdom of God is at hand" (Matthew 3:2 and 4:17). In order to become a "member" of the Kingdom, we need to end the rebellion against God where self rules and we go our own way. To be a true believer means that we come in repentance, realising that Christ died for our sins, and by faith receive salvation.

Jesus also taught that entrance into His kingdom was by "being born again". He stated that unless we are born again we cannot even see the Kingdom of God. That "new birth" had to be accomplished by the work of the Holy Spirit in making a person a spiritual being rather than just physical. Hence the Kingdom of God was very much within them. Fundamentally, it was submitting to the rule of the King – Jesus.

Jesus also made it plain that His Kingdom was like none other for He said to Pilate: "My Kingdom is not of this world. If My Kingdom were of this world, then My servants would be fighting . . ." (John 18:36). Yet, of course there was a reality about the Kingdom, for Jesus stated: "If I cast out demons by the Spirit of God, then the Kingdom of God has come upon you" (Matthew 12:28). Already the rule of God was being exercised amongst them.

It is worth noting here that Matthew's gospel usually uses the term "Kingdom of Heaven" rather than the "Kingdom of God". The Jews rightly understood that Messiah would reign on earth (we shall consider this in a later chapter), but what they failed to recognise was that Messiah would first suffer for the sins of the world, hence the cross was a stumbling block to them. They looked for a conquering hero, not a crucified Christ. Matthew, therefore, gives the Kingdom a spiritual significance, rather than a military dimension in speaking about the "Kingdom of Heaven". It took away the idea of an imminent reign on earth. It was this that Jesus was trying to correct when He told the Pharisees that the Kingdom was "not coming with signs to be observed", but that it was among them, or within them (as it can be translated).

Jesus, however, followed up His conversation with the Pharisees by talking to His disciples about the day when the Son of Man would be revealed (see Luke 17:30). The title "Son of Man" speaks not only of Jesus' humanity (as compared to the term "Son of God"), but is reminiscent of the victorious figure seen in Daniel's vision who comes on the clouds of Heaven and receives an everlasting Kingdom (see Daniel 7:13, 14). Indeed, Jesus talks about "the Son of Man coming in clouds with great power and glory" (Mark 13:26).

In Luke 17, we have recorded for us the fact that in the days leading up to His return, it would be just like the days of Noah and the days of Lot. It is interesting that He speaks of both times, because they speak of different situations, yet they both ended in judgement and destruction. Concerning the days of Noah, Jesus states that they were "drinking and marrying". They went about their daily occupations and pursuits without any thought about God.

In Genesis 6, we see the "sons of God" (usually considered to be fallen angels) taking wives from "the daughters of men". They produced the Nephilim – a tribe of giants. In other words, something other than what God had created was produced by this unnatural liaison. We might almost say that they produced monsters.

It is immediately following upon these events that we read: "Then the Lord saw the wickedness of man was great upon the earth, and that every intent of the thoughts of his heart was only evil continually." Then, having warned Noah to prepare an ark, God destroyed the earth by the flood.

At the present time, all sorts of experiments are taking place including genetic engineering and cloning. In our own nation, human cloning is limited to therapeutic cloning (i.e. the resulting embryo can be used for experiments and treating various diseases). Some us are concerned that the whole process will get out of hand and result, not in healing, but in some monstrosity. Indeed, it has already been reported that in order to produce Dolly, the sheep (a sheep cloned from its mother), hundreds of deformities were produced before they found a perfect reproduction – as they thought. Yet, even here, Dolly was not so perfect, but was old before her time, and very early on had arthritic legs and various other complaints.

When we then start to genetically manipulate plants, animals, and even humans, what will be the resulting monster? We are not God: we do not have all knowledge, neither do we fully understand the complexities of the various forms of life. It seems to me that we are overstepping the bounds of having dominion over the creatures (Genesis 1:28) to the place where we try to supersede the Creator – although mankind has long ago tried to explain away His existence through evolution. The whole process of denying God, making ourselves masters of our own destiny, manipulating life as God created it, is not only folly, but wilful rebellion against the Most High. We are inviting judgement upon ourselves! Inevitably God will bring an end to our arrogance by the return of Jesus.

God however, in His mercy, did provide a way of escape for Noah and his family by the construction of the ark. In Hebrews 11:7, we are told that it was, "By faith Noah . . . in reverence prepared an ark for the salvation of his household", and consequently received "the righteousness" which comes through faith. Noah was justified by faith; the same as every believer.

Peter, in 1 Peter 3:20, compares the passing of the ark through the floodwaters to a person passing through water in baptism. Just as Noah acted in obedience and faith in preparing the ark, so too the new believer in faith and obedience is baptised. We need to understand that New Testament baptism *always followed* faith. They never put the cart before the horse. Many times, we read similar phrases to "they believed and were baptised". As we have already seen from Hebrews, Noah and his family were saved by faith, just as the Philippian jailer and his family, for he "believed in God with his whole household" (Acts 16:34).

There is an interesting reference to Noah in 2 Peter 2:5 where it states that God "did not spare the ancient world, but preserved Noah, a preacher of righteousness, with seven others, when He brought a flood upon the world of the ungodly . . ." Noah is described as a preacher of righteousness. Clearly that righteousness is, as we have already seen, by faith. No doubt, Noah warned people of the judgement to come, and that by faith and obedience, in stepping into the ark, they could be saved. Only members of his own family heeded the call!

I find myself asking what is the situation really going to be like leading up to His return? If Jesus warned it would be like the days of Noah when people went about their activities, including being married, oblivious to God with few being saved, are we right to think of a massive end-time revival? Many proclaim that sort of scenario leading to the return of

Jesus. Frankly, I do not see it! However, what I do see is that God is gracious, and even in those days of indifference, God was seeking to make provision for people to be saved then, and will do so in these end-times. Let me say, however, if you are not yet a believer, you need to make sure of your salvation now while there is time, for the day of grace is drawing to a close.

Before we leave "the days of Noah", we might take note of the words in Matthew 24:37, 38: "For the coming of the Son of Man will be just like the days of Noah. For as in those days before the flood they were eating and drinking, marrying and giving in marriage, until the day Noah entered the ark, and they did not understand until the flood came and took them all away; so will the coming of the Son of Man be." It will be too late for so many! They will be so preoccupied with the pleasures of this life that they will miss the salvation that Jesus came to bring.

Jesus also refers to "the days of Lot" in Luke 17:28–30. In those days, said Jesus, "they were eating, they were drinking, they were buying, they were selling, they were planting, they were building; but on the day that Lot went out from Sodom it rained fire and brimstone from heaven and destroyed them all. It will be just the same on the day that the Son of Man is revealed."

It is interesting that there is no reference to marriage. We know that homosexuality was a mark of Sodom and Gomorrah. There is an interesting comment in Ezekiel 16:49f about Sodom, for it states that "she . . . had arrogance, abundant food and careless ease, but she did not help the poor and needy. Thus they were haughty and committed abominations before Me." It seems that it was out of a life of prosperity that they became arrogant and defied God.

We might observe that within our own nation, it has been with increased affluence – and arrogance towards God – that homosexuality and lesbianism has increased. When people had to toil long, hard hours to make a living, there was no time for many leisure pursuits, but as there has been more leisure time, it seems that increasingly there has been time to indulge our sinful nature more and more. Man continues to sink lower and lower. As the impact of Christianity has waned in this country, our arrogance, in assuming that we know better than God, has increased. No wonder we have seen a mushrooming of every kind of immorality with an epidemic of sexually transmitted diseases, both amongst homosexuals and heterosexuals. AIDS is still very much more prominent among homosexuals than heterosexuals in the United Kingdom.

Scripture is very plain: "You shall not lie with a male as one lies with a female; it is an abomination" (Leviticus 18:22 and similarly in 20:13). That is exactly what the men of Sodom wanted to do with the men (really, two angels) who were Lot's guests (Genesis 19:4, 5). Some try to justify such conduct by saying that their sin was promiscuous homosexuality, but that in a loving stable relationship it is different. God simply states that the act of man having sexual relationships with another man is an abomination. It is contrary to how God designed the body for sexual relations. It is to be between a man and a woman and within marriage. There are to be no other sexual relationships either prior to marriage, or outside of marriage (with a so-called partner), and certainly not with a person of the same sex. The homosexual sex acts, especially between males, are foul and a perversion of God's creation. No amount of political correctness can absolve the gross indecency or make it right in the sight of God.

Romans 1:18–26 makes it plain that because we suppress the truth (in other words, we ignore the Word of God), then there comes the time when God will give us over to promiscuity. In other words, God takes away the restraint, for He will not force us against our wills to go His way. He instructs us, and we ignore it at our peril. The passage then speaks of "degrading passions" between people of the same sex with the warning that for their indecent acts they will receive in "themselves the due penalty of their error". That may result in sexually trans-mitted diseases, but also in final judgement from God.

Paul warns the Corinthians that "the unrighteous will not inherit the Kingdom of God . . . neither fornicators (sexual relationships before marriage), nor idolaters, nor adulterers, nor effeminate (transsexuals would fit in that category), nor homosexuals, nor thieves, nor the covetous, nor drunkards, nor revilers, nor swindlers, will inherit the kingdom of God." He is able to continue by saying, however, "Such were some of you, but you were washed, but you were sanctified, but you were justified in the name of the Lord Jesus Christ and in the Spirit of our God" (1 Corinthians 6:9–11). Again, we can see that God is willing to save and forgive through faith in Christ and through His death upon the cross as He bore the penalty of our sin. However we need to see, too, that the phrase "Christian homosexual" is a contradiction in terms. You cannot become a Christian and remain a homosexual. Paul says, and "such were some of you".

Paul in writing to Timothy makes a similar point. He states that God's law has been given for "those who are lawless and rebellious . . . for murderers and immoral men and homosexuals and kidnappers and liars and perjurers and whatever else is contrary to sound teaching, according to the glorious gospel . . ." (1 Timothy 1:9–11). It is worthy of note that he not only mentions the sound teaching which the law gives regarding right and wrong conduct, but he links it with the gospel. Part of the gospel is to expose sin, so that we can go on to show, as Paul states, that "Christ Jesus came into the world to save sinners" (1 Timothy 1:15). The trouble is that, all too often, we fail to bring about a conviction of sin, because we do not expose the sin. When the Church excuses or condones homosexuality, it fails to properly preach the gospel. Scripture tells us that the law is a "tutor to lead us to Christ" (Galatians 3:24). In other words, it shows us our failure and sin, and reveals our need of a Saviour, and points us to Christ who died for our sins.

Jude reminds us that Sodom and Gomorrah "indulged in gross immorality and went after strange flesh" and are an example of "the punishment of eternal fire." Of course, all who fail to come in repentance and faith in Christ will know eternal damnation, but Sodom and Gomorrah are seen as extreme examples of sin that brought Divine retribution upon them ahead of the final judgement. We should note the reference to "strange flesh" which emphasises that this gross immorality is by its very nature something that is perverse.

There is perhaps one further Scripture which we might observe regarding the days of Lot. It is found in 2 Peter 2:7f where the apostle talks about Lot being "oppressed by the sensual conduct of unprincipled men" and that his righteous soul was "tormented day after day with their lawless deeds", but the Lord was able to preserve and rescue him.

If the final days, before the return of Christ, are to be like the days of Lot, then we can be sure that righteous believers will also be tormented by what they see. Equally, we can be sure that God is able to preserve us in the situation so that we do not succumb to the standards of others.

We need to stress here that the Church must in no way conform to the standards of the world. The whole matter of being a believer is that our minds are transformed, first through conversion and sanctification, then by the Word of God. We cannot allow the world to set our principles or our conduct no matter how coercive political correctness might be. We do no service to homosexuals to tell them that God loves them and that their conduct is acceptable. We must make them aware of their sin, and point them to the means of deliverance and salvation in Christ.

What is more, we cannot allow any practising homosexual to be a member of a church, nor exercise any ministry whether as bishops, canons, vicars or pastors. Those who do not repent must be put outside of the Church in order to bring them to repentance. That is abundantly clear from a case of immorality (not in this instance homosexuality) in 1 Corinthians 5:1–8. When we fail to make a stand on God's standards, it is little wonder that governments feel they have a green light to legalise and even promote homosexuality.

It is remarkable that Jesus should make reference to the days of Lot to indicate what life would be like prior to His return. Over recent decades we have seen homosexual relationships flourishing with the express approval of many institutions. The United Nations has championed human rights for homosexuals. From this we can see that it is a global issue. The European Union brought pressure upon the British Government to repeal and change our laws. The European Court of Human Rights made rulings which added to the pressure to change our laws. The Human Rights Convention was originally designed to prevent such abuses as were seen in the holocaust, but successive secularist judges have given ungodly rulings which defied the law of God.

Since the Blair Government came to power in 1997, we have seen a marked deterioration in moral standards. They seem to be obsessed with gay rights although that is not altogether surprising. Before Tony Blair came to power, he had supported Stonewall, a homosexual organisation, and his wife had championed gay rights within the law courts. In the first cabinet there were four homosexuals, Chris Smith (Minister for Culture), Peter Mandelson (Trade and Industry), Nick Brown (Agriculture) and Ron Davies (Welsh Secretary). It seems that the 1997 Labour election campaign was run largely by Peter Mandelson using the home of Lord Waheed Alli, a homosexual, and also director of Carlton Television. Within a year Peter Tatchell of Outrage (another homosexual group) was asked to give advice to the Government on sex education and gay rights. In the next Blair Government, Angela Mason (a lesbian and founder of Stonewall and originally a member of the Angry Brigade, an anarchist group) was put in charge of the Women's Unit in the Government.

In 1998 we became aware of plans by the Wirral Council to introduce the subject of homosexuality into sex education within its schools. At that time I was Chairman of Governors at a local high school. At a course for governors on the proposed changes, the Local Education Authority inspector for sex education informed us that they were not in breach of Clause 28 of the Local Government Act which stated that rate payers' money (now referred to as the council tax) was not to be used for "the promotion" of homosexuality. Jill Knight, a Conservative MP, had introduced a clause in to the Bill because many London boroughs were trying to show that homosexuality was a normal lifestyle. A book was being used in schools, and even pre-school play groups, called "Jenny lives with Eric and Martin". The book had a picture of a little girl in bed sitting between her father and his homosexual lover. Jill Knight's amendment was passed and put into law which restricted the homosexual lobby for many years.

In 1998, however, this local education inspector was saying that they could spread the message about homosexuality because they "were not promoting homosexuality above heterosexuality." Having followed closely the original bill, ten years before, I knew that was a distortion of what was the intention of the Act of Parliament. Consequently, I wrote to Dame Jill Knight (as she had then become) to acquaint her of what was happening. She replied: "What you have been told, quite deliberately I think, is wrong and misleading. We are aware that there is a lot of underground action aimed at nullifying Clause 28 and this is a clear indication of it. I shall report to our Family and Child Protection Group [in Parliament] what you have told me and I shall draw their attention to the public excerpts which you sent. I am shocked that an Education Department should produce an official guide for governors which they must know is wrong, and I shall, with colleagues, be taking steps on this matter."

It was not at all surprising that homosexuality was being promoted seeing Peter Tatchell was advising the Government on sex education. Also the Terrence Higgins Trust (a homosexual group as well as being linked with AIDS) was becoming involved in sex education.

Unfortunately, the Government was determined to push ahead with its gay rights agenda. By 1999, it was obvious that the Government was seeking to repeal Clause 28 and to reintroduce the Sexual Offences (Amendment Act) to lower the age of consent between homosexuals from eighteen to sixteen years of age. The Bill had been defeated in the House of Lords earlier that year. Consequently, within Intercessors For Britain, we drew up a petition to present to 10 Downing Street protesting about these moves. On the 11th October, Stewart Dool, Peter Stafford and I handed in a petition signed by almost 50,000 people against such a move. Unknown to us beforehand, on that very day, the Prime Minister was carrying out a Cabinet reshuffle. Five minutes before we handed in the petition, the Prime Minister had just re-appointed Peter Mandelson as a Cabinet Minister with responsibility for Northern Ireland. (He had resigned previously over giving false details when trying to obtain a mortgage.) We found the timing most significant because, along with the petition, we had handed in a leaflet outlining the biblical position on homosexuality. We felt that it was, in effect, a rebuke from the Lord.

The only response we received from the Government to our petition was that they were seeking to create "a fair and tolerant society". Obviously God's laws meant nothing to the Prime Minister or other Cabinet Ministers. By the end of 2000, the Government had passed the Sexual Offences Act by using the Parliament Act, and in 2003, Clause 28 was repealed. During that same year, Parliament passed a bill allowing gay couples to adopt, and in spite of reassurances from the Prime Minister to some Labour MPs that gay adoption would not be allowed, he voted in favour of it.

The Government was clearly determined to push through its agenda of gay rights. Journalists have commented that everything the gay lobby requested by way of reform, the Government has granted. Government directives have meant that the police have had to appoint a diversity officer who is responsible, amongst others things, to make sure there is the right balance of homosexual officers to heterosexual officers as is found in the population generally. (The homosexuals claimed that they are ten per cent of the population, whereas most surveys claim it is fewer than one per cent.) The same policy applies to the Fire Service. Teachers, after the repeal of Clause 28, have been ordered to take "sexuality training" to give them a better understanding of homosexual issues.

In 2005 the Civil Partnership Act took effect, giving to homosexual couples the same rights as married couples in terms of housing, pension rights, next of kin etc. We also saw the Gender Recognition Bill being accepted as law, allowing transsexuals who were born male to change their birth certificate to female, and vice versa. Anybody who discloses a person's true sex can be fined £5,000; and a clergyman who refuses to marry such a person can also be fined. (The Government has given some assurances that secondary legislation will be permitted to give some protection in the case of ordination, church membership and marriage, but to date no such moves have taken place.) What seems so appalling is the fraudulent nature of re-registering a birth certificate with what is in fact a lie. It shows us how depraved we have become. This Government has encouraged homosexuality and perversion in a way that is almost unbelievable.

On top of that, television with its various "soap operas" has sought to make homosexuality acceptable. Various Gay Pride weeks and festivals have brought its perversion out on to our streets, and instead of hanging their head in shame, they flaunt their homosexuality. Gay clubs and gay villages, such as in Manchester, mean that those righteous souls like Lot are tormented by what they see. Sex education encourages teenagers to experiment with their sexuality, and yet, in the past, it was recognised that youngsters, until they reached puberty, were drawn more to children of their own sex, but the reverse took place as they grew older.

We have "sown the wind and reaped the whirlwind" as Hosea said. Our time can most certainly be described as being like "the days of Lot." Clearly, this is another indication that the time for the Lord's return is near. Fifty years ago, no one could have imagined such a description would fit our day. Even when in 1967, homosexual acts in private between consenting adults (twenty-one years of age) was no longer an offence, no one would have expected such a major change in the moral outlook. What is more, this is not just a national matter, but a worldwide phenomenon.

Again, we should note that the days of Lot were marked by ungodliness and total disregard of God. It is far from a time of revival leading up to the return of Jesus, as so many seem to indicate. In fact we can go further because Jesus asked the question, "When the Son of Man comes, will He find faith (literally, 'the faith') on the earth?" (Luke 18:8).

I should point out that there are no chapter divisions in the original Greek, therefore, we tend to miss sometimes the link between one chapter and another. Luke 17:20–37 is all about the return of Jesus. The first part of chapter 18 is still related to the second coming, hence the question about His return to earth. Verse 8 concludes this section with the parable about the "unjust judge" and the woman's persistence in coming to get justice. The purpose of the parable is to show that we "ought to pray" at all times "and not to lose heart." Jesus commends the persistence of the woman in making her request to the judge. He contrasts the lack of response from the judge with the willingness of God to "bring about justice for them quickly" (v. 8). He then asks the question about whether there will be (the) faith on the earth at His return.

My understanding of the passage as a whole (chapters 17 and 18) is that the time will come when we "will long to see one of the days of the Son of Man" (17:22), but those days of power will be missing. Instead, it will be like the times of Noah and Lot; people will be oblivious to God, and wickedness will mark the days prior to His return. How are we going to face such a time? Only by praying at all times, otherwise we shall be discouraged. Our appeal to God for justice will really be a matter of pleading for vindication, and of deliverance from antichrist himself. Christians are going to be persecuted. It may even be that as a result of what I have written in this chapter, I may be prosecuted, at some later stage, for so-called "hate crimes" against homosexuals. Let me say that I believe warning homosexuals and pointing them to salvation in Christ is a loving thing to do, but the courts might still find one guilty. What do we do? We take our appeal to the highest Court in the universe – the Court of Heaven. God will indeed vindicate His own by the return of Jesus. The question is, however "When the Son of Man comes will He find *the* faith on the earth?" Yes, if we pray constantly looking to God for strength.

Again, we notice the importance of prayer linked with the end-times. We cannot stand in our own strength. Like the disciples of old, we need to watch and pray lest we enter into temptation.

CHAPTER FOUR

APOSTASY AND LAWLESSNESS

> With regard to the coming of our Lord Jesus Christ and our gathering together to Him. . . . Let no one in any way deceive you, for it will not come unless the apostasy comes first, and the man of lawlessness is revealed . . . . (2 Thessalonians 2:1–3)

I have already hinted that the assumption many have regarding a massive end-time revival, before the return of Christ, is not scriptural. The Scriptures clearly warn of a falling away from the faith as being the hallmark of the days leading up to Christ's return. In the above quote, Paul states that an apostasy will take place first. Jesus also warns that prior to His return many would fall away and that the love of many would grow cold (Matthew 24:10–12).

There are many reasons why the Church ignores the warnings of deception and apostasy as signs of the closing age. First of all, people prefer to look at the future through rose-coloured spectacles rather than face a rather unpleasant prospect.

Secondly, they read that God will pour out His Spirit in the last days. Peter saw that being fulfilled at Pentecost, for the last days began then and will continue until the return of Jesus. The Holy Spirit has never been withdrawn, and without His activity people can never be born again. Yet, however, there have been times, in Church history, when there have been little evident signs of progress, especially in the Middle Ages. Even in those heady days of the Acts of the Apostles, Stephen, who was full of the Holy Spirit when addressing the Sanhedrin, did not find a very positive response. Although the Council could not withstand the wisdom of Stephen, given by the Holy Spirit, they rejected his message and stoned him to death! The Holy Spirit was at work, but they resisted. That has been the situation in much of Church history. It depends as much upon the hearts of the hearers as it does on the activity of the Holy Spirit.

Thirdly, people believe that the gospel will have such an influence that the whole world will be Christianised. They support their views by referring to the parable concerning leaven. Jesus talked about a woman hiding leaven among three measures of flour until all was leavened. They wrongly interpret this to mean that the whole world will be permeated by the gospel of Christ until all the world is Christianised. The reality is somewhat different!

First of all, flour represents something that is pure, but leaven always represents evil. Leaven was never to be offered up to God in sacrifice, but the flour could. Jesus warned His disciples to "beware of the leaven of the Pharisees and Sadducees." Eventually they realised that He was warning them against the teaching of these two groups, for they both invalidated Scripture. The former did so by adding to Scripture their oral tradition, while the latter rejected the prophets and the writings (Matthew 16:6 and 12).

Paul twice used the statement, "A little leaven leavens the whole lump." In the first instance, he was warning the Corinthian Church that immorality left unchecked would contaminate the whole assembly (1 Corinthians 5:6). In the second case, he warns the Galatian churches that trying to be justified by works (such as circumcision and the keeping of the law) rather than being justified by faith was an attitude that would corrupt the churches. Leaven is, therefore, seen as a malevolent influence rather than a Christianising influence.

Added to that, we notice that the women hid the leaven. The gospel is not to be hidden: it is to be proclaimed outwardly. There is something sinister about craftily hiding the leaven. Jesus is, therefore, warning that the purity of the gospel will be contaminated.

Again, Church history would show that to be the case. It is not politically correct, in these days of ecumenical engagement, to point the finger at Catholicism but the fact remains that the Catholic Church proclaims that "the sacraments are the chief means of salvation." Attendance at the mass, paying penance, carrying out indulgences, and engaging in good works are all necessary for salvation according to Catholic teaching. This can be verified very easily by examining the Catechism of that Church.

They speak of a special priesthood whereas Scripture speaks of the priesthood of all believers. They forbid their priests from being married whereas Scripture teaches it is perfectly wholesome and that any prohibition may result in immorality – something which has been seen all too often in the abuse of children. They proclaim transubstantiation (a change of substance of the bread into the body of Christ, and the wine into blood) whereas the Bible speaks of eating bread and drinking wine.

The whole hierarchical system such as is found in the Catholic Church is completely absent in the New Testament. From Acts 20, we see that bishops were simply elders of a local Church. Nowhere in Scripture do we find evidence for the papacy; after all Paul opposed Peter to his face (Galatians 2:11). Neither is the concept of papal infallibility found in the Bible. Scripture, however, does warn of the dangers of deception and that we need to "test the spirits to see whether they are from God" (1 John 4:1). I believe that if Catholicism were emerging today, we would describe it as a cult because it is so far removed from the origins of the faith as described in the Bible. They, like the Pharisees, have added their traditions to Scripture. Beware of the leaven!

It was, therefore, a triumph for the gospel when the Reformation began with its emphasis on "justification by faith" and a return to the Bible for our teaching. For several hundred years, after the Reformation, we saw a return to the Word in an attempt to recover the original truth. Unfortunately, we have seen a subtle return to the quiet influence of leaven. Deception has come in a much more subtle form. The Word of Faith movement has distorted faith, and as part of its message proclaimed a prosperity gospel which is contrary to Christ's message of laying up treasure in heaven. Some of us have seen the whole work of prayer and intercession corrupted by non-biblical practices. The apostasy is spreading.

Once again, we are listening to the teachings of men instead of holding to the teaching of Scripture.

When I look back on my own conversion and the grounding that I had in Scripture, and I see some of the things that are said and done today, I find myself utterly dismayed at how far many of the evangelical and charismatic churches have moved away from the truth. The spiritual decline in understanding the truth has run parallel with the moral decline in our nation.

Deception will be a major problem leading up to the return of Christ. Jesus, in speaking about the end, warned that false prophets and messiahs (anointed ones) together with false signs and wonders would be prevalent before His return (see Matthew 24, Mark 13 and Luke 21). These would become so marked that even the elect might be deceived, Jesus warned.

Paul states that in later times seducing spirits and doctrines of demons would cause people to *fall away* from the faith (1 Timothy 4:1). He also warns that not only perilous times would come, leading up to the return, but that standards of decency, conduct and morality would decline. Selfishness and self-centredness would rule the day. He warns, too, that evil men and impostors would "proceed from bad to worse, deceiving and being deceived" (see 2 Timothy 3, especially v. 13). The only thing which can prevent us from being deceived, as he shows, is to be grounded in the Scriptures which are God-inspired and can adequately equip the people of God (vv. 16 and 17).

If we return to 2 Thessalonians 2 and the quote at the beginning of this chapter, we see that Paul makes clear that

Jesus will not return until the apostasy first takes place, but also that the man of lawlessness is to be revealed. The Authorised Version talks about the "man of sin", but "sin is lawlessness" according to 1 John 3:4. The AV follows certain Greek manuscripts, while other translations follow alternative manuscripts. However, they all go on to speak about "the mystery of lawlessness" and "the lawless one" in 2 Thessalonians 2:7, 8.

The Greek word for lawlessness is *anomia,* coming from *nomos* meaning law. When Paul talks about the law, he will have in mind the Hebrew equivalent which is *torah*. It comes from a Hebrew root meaning "to teach". Therefore, the concept behind the scriptural use of "law" is that of instruction. Basically, the law of God is the instruction of God. The man of lawlessness is, therefore, one who is opposed to God's instruction. The "mystery of lawlessness" is that evil force which is at work in the world which undermines God's teaching and God's ways. From 2 Thessalonians 2, we see that Satan lies behind this work of lawlessness and the man of lawlessness who is also known as the antichrist.

There are those who follow an interpretation arising from some of the Reformers who say that the "man of lawlessness" is the papacy. While I have some sympathy with that position, especially bearing in mind some of the titles that the papacy holds, nevertheless, Paul talks of the *man* of lawlessness (singular) – not *men* of lawlessness. Also Jesus, on His return, destroys this *man* (2 Thessalonians 2:3, 8).

I would also want to link this passage in 2 Thessalonians 2 with Daniel 7:25 which refers to the one who will speak out "against the Most High and will wear down the saints", and who will make "alterations in times and in law (*torah*)." This person emerges from a fourth kingdom. There are three kingdoms which have gone before. Both from Daniel 2 and Daniel 7, we can see the order, starting with the Babylonian, Persian, Greek and fourthly, the Roman Empire. In Daniel 2, it is in this fourth Kingdom (the Roman) that an eternal Kingdom comes into existence with the birth of Jesus in Bethlehem. From Daniel 7, we see that one arises out of this fourth kingdom (the Roman Empire) who will make changes in law and times.

In Revelation 17:8 it talks of "the beast" (antichrist) as having previously existed ("was"), then disappearing ("is not"), but then came to life again ("is about to come up out of the abyss"). The European Union claims to be a revival of the Roman Empire with the treaty of Rome, and the EU Constitution being signed alongside the ruins of the Roman Forum in Rome.

It is interesting how much the EU is tied to Catholicism. Let me mention one item and that is the European flag. The ring of twelve stars on the flag was taken from a stylised halo of a picture of the virgin Mary displayed in Strasbourg.

The main point, however, in referring to Daniel 7 is that an arrogant leader who speaks out against God, also seeks to make changes in law (*torah* or *nomos*). Surely, therefore this is why in the New Testament, he is called "the lawless one".

There are other links that are often not recognised. In Matthew 24:10–13, Jesus warns that many will fall away, and that false prophets will mislead many prior to His return. Then He adds: "Because *lawlessness* (AV "iniquity", but the Greek is *anomia* – the same as in 2 Thessalonians 2) is increased, most people's love will grow cold. But the one who endures to the end, he will be saved."

There are two things to note here: first, the warnings of falling away and the need to endure. The matter of one's love growing cold clearly has to do with love of the Lord, and therefore the importance of endurance if we are to be saved. That vital point is overlooked by many evangelicals.

The second point to note is that the falling away and coldness towards the Lord is linked to lawlessness increasing. One thing ought to be abundantly clear in combining Matthew 24 and 2 Thessalonians 2 and that is that an evil influence is at work in the world. 2 Thessalonians 2 talks about a restraint being taken away, so that the man of lawlessness can appear. Therefore, prior to the antichrist (man of lawlessness) coming on the scene, opposition to God's instruction and ways will increase. Once he has appeared, it will get even worse, because he will make changes in law (*torah*). The net result will be that because the world has so abandoned the ways of God, believers could become dejected and renounce the faith they once endorsed, especially if persecution increases and trading becomes impossible (as Revelation indicates).

Putting these passages together (Daniel, Matthew and 2 Thessalonians), we see that the trends in society will be such that all biblical morals will be increasingly abandoned. It is worth noting here how we, and so many nations, have moved away from biblical standards of conduct. Witchcraft and homosexuality have been permitted and encouraged by a change of law. Capital punishment has been repealed. Sunday trading has been permitted. Marriage has been debased by this Government with Patricia Hewitt (when Minister for Trade and Industry) stating that marriage has no place in modern Britain. The family is no longer regarded to consist solely of a married couple with children, but also unmarried parents, or even homosexual parents and children. As we have already seen, homosexuality has become rampant in our society.

Faith in the one true God has been undermined by the Blair Government's emphasis on multiculturalism. The new millennium was marked by Tony Blair presiding over a multi-faith meeting of the leaders of the various world religions in this country. What an insult to the One who gave His life for us, especially as the new millennium marked His coming into the world two thousand years ago.

It has become politically incorrect to any longer proclaim that Jesus is the only way to God. The United Nations has brought its influence to bear here by stating that all religions are of equal value. In so many ways lawlessness has increased, paving the way for the man of lawlessness to appear.

There are two further points I need to cover before we leave this subject. First of all, it should be noted that Paul states not only that the apostasy will take place before the return of Jesus, but that the man of lawlessness will be revealed and will exalt himself above every so-called god, and will take "his seat in the temple of God, displaying himself as being God" (2 Thessalonians 2:4). I do not intend to enter into the debate about whether the phrase "the temple of God" refers to a rebuilt temple in Jerusalem, or to some exalted place within Christendom (e.g. St Peter's in Rome, as some would suggest). What I do want to emphasise, however, is that the man of lawlessness will be recognised and give himself an exalted position. Paul shows that the apostasy and the appearance of antichrist are the final indications that the Lord's return is near.

The other matter, and here again I stand on the dangerous ground of theological debate, relates to the words: "you know what restrains him [the man of lawlessness] now." In other words, something is hindering the appearance of the man of lawlessness until the appointed time.

There has been much debate as to what this means ranging from the Roman Empire, to the Church or the Holy Spirit being removed. The first group believes that while the Roman Empire was strong and under the authority of the Emperor, the man of lawlessness (in their interpretation, the papacy) could not be exalted. Others believe it is the Church which is restraining him, but when the church is raptured, then the restraint is taken away. They believe that with the removal of the Church, the Holy Spirit is also removed. Such people believe in what is called "a pre-tribulation rapture" (i.e. the Church, consisting of true believers will not face the tribulation, but will be caught up to meet the Lord in the air *prior* to the tribulation).

It is not my purpose at this point to debate when believers will be caught up to meet the Lord, but clearly it cannot happen prior to the man of lawlessness being revealed and setting himself up as a god. Why do I say that? Because Paul states that "the coming of our Lord Jesus Christ and our gathering together to Him" will not take place until the man of lawlessness is revealed (2 Thessalonians 2:1–3). As I have already mentioned, some argue that it is the rapture of the Church (and the removal of the Holy Spirit) which removes that restraint and allows the man of lawlessness to be revealed. However Paul makes it plain that believers will not be "raptured" until the man of lawless is revealed. Therefore, the Church will still be here when the lawless one comes on the scene. If that is the case, then we have to be ready for increasing lawlessness, especially leading up to the appearance of antichrist. That is the main point I want to make here.

My personal opinion is that God has appointed an angel to hold back lawlessness, for it talks about "*he* who now restrains" (v. 7). We can see in the Book of Revelation, and in other Scriptures, that the angels hold back the powers of darkness, and even bind Satan for a thousand years (Revelation 20:1f).

While that may be a matter of debate, we, in the leadership of Intercessors For Britain together with many other intercessors, felt that something of restraint had been removed when Tony Blair's government was elected in 1997. We felt that something had happened in the heavenlies and, where previously we had seen much evil held back we were now seeing lawlessness increasing. It certainly took a major leap forward as we saw a moral, spiritual and cultural change take place. I believe that we are in the "run-up" to the man of lawlessness being revealed.

I would plead with you not to be so locked into a theological position that you are ill-prepared for the things coming upon the earth. The Scripture is plain that the love of many will grow cold because lawlessness is increased on the earth. It will be like the days of Noah and Lot before His return. Do not be deceived; those who state otherwise are false prophets. If they claim to have an anointing and proclaim a different situation, then they are false christs (false anointed ones).

Be careful that you do not allow the situation, as it arises, to cause you to lose heart, and turn away from the One who saved you! Jesus gave us warning in advance so that we might be ready. Again, I would remind you that He stated, "Men ought always to pray and not lose heart" (Luke 18:1).

CHAPTER FIVE

SPIRITUAL BATTLES

The Christian has always faced spiritual battles. As Paul reminds us: "Our struggle is not against flesh and blood, but against the rulers, against the powers, against the world forces of this darkness, against the spiritual forces of wickedness in the heavenly places" (Ephesians 6:12). These battles, however, are likely to become more acute as this age draws to a close. Revelation 12 ends with the statement: ". . . the dragon was enraged with the woman, and went off to make war with the rest of her children, who keep the commandments of God and hold to the testimony of Jesus."

There are several areas where the battle will be fierce. The first concerns Israel. We have already seen that Jesus indicated that Israel would be restored, with Jerusalem under Jewish control again. Zechariah 12 shows a time when Jerusalem would become "a cup that causes reeling to all the peoples around" and that it would also be "a heavy stone for all the peoples; all who lift it will be severely injured." There is no doubt that Jerusalem is a contentious issue with the Palestinians wanting it as their capital while Israel has declared that it is their eternal capital. It is certain that all peace talks will founder on this issue of Jerusalem. Zechariah, therefore, foretells that all the nations will come against Jerusalem.

When the UN partitioned the land, and Israel came into being in 1948, many of the Arab nations attacked the Jews who had been living in the Jewish quarter of the walled city. As a result, the Jews were driven out of Jerusalem. When it was recaptured in 1967 with the so-called West Bank, the Arab population – especially the Muslims – were devastated. For them it was a disaster. They are determined to regain, not only Jerusalem and the West Bank, but also to conquer the whole area, including Tel Aviv and Haifa. Back in 1948, the Arab forces were going to drive the Jews into the sea, and that is still their aim. Jerusalem is going to be like a drug or poisoned chalice to those round about, and a heavy stone that will injure all who try to lift it.

In the end, the nations will try, by force, to find a solution. They will engage the Jewish forces, but Zechariah says that at that point God "will pour out on the House of David and on the inhabitants of Jerusalem, the Spirit of grace and supplication, so that they will look on Me (in Hebrew literally, "look to Me") whom they have pierced . . ." It states that as a result of a time of mourning over the One that they have pierced, a fountain for cleansing sin and impurity will be opened for the House of David and Jerusalem (see Zechariah 12:1 – 13:1). Many believe that this fits exactly with what Paul speaks about regarding the hardness of heart being removed and all Israel being saved, once the fullness of the Gentiles has been brought in – i.e. the major work of missionary witness to the nations of the world (Romans 11:25, 26).

If Zechariah 12 – 14 are in chronological order, then their turning to the Lord clearly comes before the second coming of Jesus where He descends and stands on the Mount of Olives (14:4). We see from this, therefore, that the salvation of Israel is to take place prior to the return of Jesus.

We have already noticed from Revelation 12 that Satan makes war on the woman with the rest of her children (literally, "seed"), who keep the commandments of God and hold to the testimony of Jesus. The latter is clear: Satan is going to declare war on Christians. The first part is less so. Who is the "woman"? Catholics will point to Mary, but many evangelicals believe this to be Israel for the woman is clothed with the sun and moon and has twelve stars. It is reminiscent of Joseph's dream with the sun, moon (his parents) and eleven stars (Joseph being the twelfth) bowing down before him. This was where the Israelites began with Jacob and his twelve sons. If, therefore, we see that the woman represents Israel, then we understand that Satan makes war with the Jewish people and with true believers in the Lord Jesus Christ.

Satan has declared war on God's two elect peoples. That makes perfect sense if Satan is God's adversary. Where God sets apart a people for Himself, then Satan will contest it. It is surely this that explains anti-Semitism. This has to be the explanation of the holocaust and Hitler's final solution. It was demonically inspired. There is no other satisfactory explanation.

Yet it is not simply Nazism that wanted to exterminate all Jews, that is also the intention of Islam, as we saw in Chapter 2.

The world fails to appreciate the real problem in the Middle East. It is not a battle between two peoples for the land, but it is a battle in which Islam cannot accept a Jewish state, nor the existence of the Jewish race. During the Second World War the Grand Mufti of Jerusalem (the supreme Muslim leader in the area) gave full endorsement to Hitler's final solution. It accords fully with the theology of Islam.

Here is one of the major spiritual battles that we see leading up to the return of Jesus the Messiah. Surely Satan must hate everything about Jews. For a start, Jesus was a Jew, and "salvation is from the Jews", as Jesus Himself stated. The way was prepared by Moses and the Jewish prophets who foretold the birth of Jesus (a descendant of David, a Jew) and His death. The apostles were all Jews, and the Scriptures were written by Jews under the inspiration of God. It would seem too that there comes a point when the nation of Israel will come to repentance and faith in Christ. This has to happen prior to the return of Jesus. Therefore, war is declared on the Jews to exterminate them in the holocaust, and then subsequently to prevent them from returning to the land of Israel. At a later stage, as we have already seen, Jerusalem will become a problem to the world ("a cup of reeling" and "a heavy stone" for all the nations), so that they attack it. That will be the point of their salvation. No wonder Satan wants their destruction!

Ezekiel prophesies a time when God will bring the Jews back from the nations after being scattered among the nations. God states that He will then wash them with clean water, give them a new heart and put His Spirit in them (Ezekiel 36). The next chapter speaks of dead bones coming together and life being breathed into them. God would bring them out of their graves.

In 1947, when Masada was being excavated, a fragment of the prophecy of Ezekiel was found. It was Ezekiel 37:11–14 which speaks of the bones of the house of Israel being dried up and their hope perished, but that God would open their graves and bring them into the land of Israel. God would put His Spirit within them and they would come to life. Masada was the place where the last Jews held out against the Romans after the destruction of Jerusalem in AD 70. They committed suicide en masse rather than fall into the hands of the Romans. Masada was a graveyard! Just one year after that fragment of Ezekiel was found, the state of Israel was reborn in 1948. An army of dead bones had, in effect, come to life and been brought back into the land. We might also add that the restoration of Israel also arose from the graves of the holocaust. There is no doubt that gave special impetus to the birth of the state of Israel. If they were to avoid a similar destruction, they must find a land where they could live and be safe. Their natural destiny was the British Mandate of Palestine. Although many were turned back by British Troops, many succeeded in getting into the land, and many holocaust survivors ended up in Israel.

To return to Ezekiel 37, the prophet speaks of two sticks being joined together and becoming one. The House of Judah (the Southern Kingdom) was to be joined to Ephraim and all the House of Israel (the Northern Kingdom). They were not, however, reunited after their return from exile in Babylon. What had been the Northern Kingdom was populated by a mixed race that became known as the Samaritans which remained to the time of Jesus, with Israel finally being destroyed in AD 70.

The two Kingdoms have never been reunited since they split after Solomon's death. That, however, is exactly what God showed Ezekiel was going to happen. While there are still the problems concerning the West Bank, nevertheless territory which was once part of the Northern Kingdom of Israel is now reunited within the Southern Kingdom of Judah in the modern state of Israel. The prophecy has been fulfilled except that it goes on to speak of them having one king over them namely, "My servant David. . . . And they will all have one Shepherd. . . ." We shall consider this aspect later.

Surely Satan will contest this all of this, and especially those events tied up with the salvation of Israel. In chapter 38, Ezekiel prophesies that "in the last days" (v. 16), God will bring up "Gog of the land of Magog", the chief prince of Rosh, together with Meshech and Tubal against Israel at a time when Israel is at peace and living securely (A similar war takes place, too, at the end of the Millennium – see Revelation 20:8). Meshech and Tubal were tribes which settled in the region of Turkey. Others come up who are in alliance with this ruler namely, Gomer, Beth-togarmah (linked with Turkey, the Crimean region and Southern Russia), and from the remote parts of the North (which could be Russia or those Muslim areas that once formed part of USSR). It also mentions Persia (modern Iran), Cush (Ethiopia and Sudan) and Put (usually recognised as Libya). The interesting thing is that all those nations are Muslim today. There is not a single point in history when all of these nations have come against Israel, but Islam's hatred of Israel is likely to bring them together to fight against Israel, especially if Jerusalem remains under Jewish control.

The outcome of this battle is that God defends Israel and the attacking forces are destroyed by God. As a result God's name will be magnified and sanctified among those nations and they will know that he is "the LORD (Yahweh)." It is not the name of Allah that will be great, but the God of Israel – and the God and Father of our Lord Jesus Christ. Many of us feel that this battle with Israel will result in many Muslims deserting their faith and coming to recognise the God of Israel, and what He sought to do through His Son in saving the world.

An acquaintance of mine who was living in Amman, Jordan, when Israel recaptured Jerusalem in 1967 told me that the Muslims were shattered by Israel's victory. They asked, "Why has Allah allowed this?" Surely a greater victory for Israel, in the "Magog War", against overwhelming numerical odds, would bring about a greater disillusionment, and an opportunity to proclaim the gospel to Muslims as never before.

However, after Israel's victory in 1967, the Ayatollah Khomeni, who led the revolt against the Shah of Persia, declared that the Muslims would gain the victory when there was a perfect Muslim state. His influence brought about a resurgence of Islam, not only in Iran, but throughout the Middle East. He referred to Israel as "Satan" and America as "Greater Satan", because of its support for Israel because he maintained it was not God who brought Israel into being, but Satan. (At least the Ayatollah understood that the rebirth of Israel was a supernatural event, unlike some Christians!)

In the light of this, we can understand why America was singled out for the destruction of the twin towers in New York by militant Muslims on 11th September 2001. Osama Bin Laden who, almost certainly, was the mastermind behind that attack had declared war on America mainly because he objected to "infidel (American) troops" on Saudi soil during the first Gulf war. He was incensed that these infidels should be allowed on Muslim territory – to protect Saudi Arabia from a possible attack by Saddam Hussein in the light of his conquest of Kuwait. It was on the eighth anniversary of American troops going into Saudi Arabia that the US embassies in Kenya and Tanzania were targeted with many losing their lives.

We should not think that Islam is only concerned about Israel though. Islamic theology may speak of "peace", but it only exists for Muslims. You are either in "the house of peace" (i.e. Muslims), or "the house of war" (non-Muslims). Upon such infidels – not simply those who convert from Islam – but on all non-Muslims, jihad (holy war) is declared. Moderate Muslims may interpret that as propaganda – an attempt to convert the West to Islam – but others will see it in a very different light!

We, in Britain, are largely ignorant of the intentions of many Muslims, especially the imams. Their policy, outlined in a book published in 1980 called *Muslim Communities in Non-Muslim States*, is that they will gather in Muslim enclaves and avoid being integrated into the society around them. They will then seek to become a majority in a given area and then demand the same religious and political rights as other groups. Once these have been gained they will seek to impose their way of life upon the whole nation. Some of our major towns are very close to being controlled by Muslim majorities. We may wake up when it is too late. David Pawson has stated that he believes God showed him that our nation would become Muslim, mainly because the Church has been asleep.

It may not be too late. I believe that ultimately Israel will bring about the demise of Islam, but it will be a major spiritual battle. We need to be careful that we recognise this to be a spiritual battle against forces of darkness. While many militant Muslims may be fighting for the heart of our nation, they are controlled by those powers of darkness. In love, we need to pray that they may come to faith in Christ. Jesus died for them as much as any other group of people. They are in bondage (Islam means "submission"), having to obey the five pillars of Islam: prayer five times a day; fasting during daylight hours in Ramadan; making haj (pilgrimage) to Mecca; repeating the creed ("there is no god but Allah and Mohammed is his prophet"), and giving to charity.

Al-jazeera television expressed concern about the number of Muslims becoming Christians in Africa. It was stated that "In every hour, 667 Muslims convert to Christianity. Every day, 16,000 Muslims convert to Christianity. Every year, 6 million Muslims convert to Christianity." It would seem that more and more Muslims are put off by the violence which the religion encourages, the ritual of praying five times a day, the fasting, and reciting verses from the Koran that are meaningless to them.

We should, therefore, be encouraged by these trends, but I believe major battles lie ahead of us. I believe that it is by prayer that we shall prevail. We need to acknowledge the sinfulness of our own nation which leaves us ripe for takeover by Islam. We need to acknowledge the failure of the Church to hold to God's instruction, or to understand that we are fighting demonic forces here. The Church has been asleep while an enemy has been sowing the seeds of dissension and destruction. We have failed to pray for the salvation of Muslims or to witness to them. We have been intimidated by their militancy and by political correctness which declares that all religions are of equal value.

Eventually, the powers in the heavens will be shaken, especially by the return of Christ, but it is time for the Christian to put on the whole armour of God that we might stand against the wiles of Satan. That armour is given so that we might resist the forces of darkness by our prayers and our proclamation of the gospel. Both prayer and preaching are essential.

The hottest battle, however, will not be over Britain, but over Israel. All hell will be let loose. I believe that was the case in the holocaust, but the final onslaught will be by Islam against Israel. Islam calls for nothing less than the total destruction of Israel.

My colleague, Stewart Dool and I with our wives, were at an international intercessors meeting in Israel in September 2000 – at the very time the last intifada began. During the week, a representative from the mayor of Jerusalem's office spoke to us. He stated that the problem which they faced was not a problem with the Palestinians, but with Islam. They could make peace with the Palestinians if it were not for Islam. We, as intercessors, recognised the absolute truth of that statement.

Since then we have seen an increase in suicide bombings which have been encouraged by Hamas. In the elections which took place in the Palestinian Authority in January 2006, Hamas gained the majority of seats giving them outright control. The Charter of Hamas shows that there is no place for Israel, for it states: "Israel will rise and will remain erect until Islam eliminates it as it had eliminated its predecessors." It continues by saying, "Hamas believes the land of Palestine [to them that means the Palestinian areas and the whole of Israel] has been an Islamic Waqf [land] throughout the generations and until the Day of Resurrection, no one can renounce it or part of it, or abandon it or part of it . . . Hamas is a distinct Palestinian Movement which owes its loyalty to Allah, derives from Islam its way of life and strives to raise the banner of Allah over every inch of Palestine." The Charter also states: "When our enemies usurp some Islamic lands, Jihad becomes a duty binding on all Muslims. In order to face the usurpation of Palestine by the Jews, we have no escape from raising the banner of Jihad."

They have talked of the possibility of a truce with Israel, but only until they are strong enough to eradicate the Jewish state. This is a typical Muslim ploy which was used by Mohammed himself.

In October 2005, Mahmoud Ahmadinejad, President of Iran, made a number of speeches calling for Israel to be "wiped off the map" and describing the holocaust as a "myth". He later stated that this had a profound effect upon the Muslim world providing the "shock" that was needed "to awaken the Muslims who are in a state of lethargy." Then he added: "Some in Iran and abroad thought that we were making these speeches without a specific plan and policy, but we have been pursuing a specific strategy in this regard." "The revival of Islam is whipping the frail body of the Global Hegemon", Ahmadinejad said in a reference to the United States. "This global hegemon will soon be toppled" (*Iran Focus*, 3 January 2006).

A month later, addressing the hundreds of thousands who turned out to mark the twenty-seventh anniversary of the Islamic Revolution, President Ahmadinejad said: "We ask the West to remove what they created sixty years ago and if they do not listen to our recommendations, the Palestinian nation and other nations will eventually do this for them. Remove Israel before it is too late and save yourself from the fury of the regional nations" (*WorldNetDaily*).

During the recent conflict between Israel and Hizbollah (July/August 2006) the president of Iran made a similar statement saying, "The real cure for the conflict is elimination of the Zionist regime." There is no doubt that Hizbollah is supported by Iran as well as Syria, and that Iran is already fighting against Israel through its proxy, Hizbollah, who over a period of six years had regularly fired katyusha rockets into northern Israel.

With Iran developing nuclear power and possibly nuclear weapons, the threats from Ahmadinejad have continued. After announcing the "atomic miracle" of producing enriched uranium, he stated (in April 2006): "Like it or not, the Zionist regime is heading towards annihilation . . . The Zionist regime is a rotten, dried tree that will be eliminated by one storm."

What is worse, the president of Iran believes that he has a divine mission. Shi'ites believe that the twelfth descendant of Mohammed, known as the twelfth Imam or the Mahdi, went into "grand occultation", or hiding in 941, and that he is hidden in the well in Jamkaran, Iran, and that his return will coincide with an apocalyptic battle between the forces of evil and righteousness, with evil being ultimately routed. Mahmoud Ahmadinejad claimed that, as he addressed the United Nations in September 2005, the "Hidden Imam drenched the place in a sweet light." He has also stated that "Our revolution's main mission is to pave the way for the reappearance of the twelfth Imam, the Mahdi. We should define our economic, cultural and political policies on the policy of the Imam Mahdi's return."

From other statements Ahmadinejad has made, he believes that 2007 will be the year of the Mahdi's appearance and that a period of chaos will proceed that event. Nuclear weapons in his hand could well be the means of promoting such chaos thus creating the very conditions to bring about the appearance of the hidden Imam as the Iranian President sees it. Even without nuclear weapons, he is already causing chaos in Iraq by encouraging the insurgency. If it leads to civil war in Iraq, which is probably his intention, then Saudi Arabia as well as Iran could be drawn into a new Gulf war as those two countries come to the aid of the Shi'ites on the one hand (Iran) and Sunnis on the other (Saudi Arabia).

There can be no doubt that with the elections of the Iranian President in 2005 and Hamas within the Palestinian territories in 2006, we are nearing the time when Ezekiel 38 and 39 will be fulfilled. President Ahmadinejad sees himself at war with Israel and the West as well, believing in Islam's ultimate conquest of the world.

Regarding the threat to Israel, we need to understand that such attempts by the evil one to eliminate Israel have always been in his mind. Psalm 83 sums up the ancient enmity towards God's chosen people: "They make shrewd plans against Your people, and conspire together against Your treasured ones. They have said, 'Come, and let us wipe them out as a nation, that the name of Israel be remembered no more' " (vv. 3, 4). It is perhaps worth remembering that the Psalm ends by saying, ". . . pursue them with Your tempest and terrify them with Your storm. Fill their faces with dishonour that they may seek Your name, O LORD (literally *Yahweh* – not Allah). Let them be ashamed and dismayed forever, and let them be humiliated and perish, that they may know that You alone, whose name is the LORD (*Yahweh*), are the Most High over all the earth."

We pray that, in the end, those Islamic nations which set their face against Israel may indeed recognise that the God of Abraham, Isaac and Jacob (Israel) is the one true God, and that He sent His Son for the salvation of the world. We seek the salvation of those Muslim nations. This is part of the spiritual battle that we must wage – but remember it is not against flesh and blood, but against principalities and powers.

The second major area of conflict will concern the Church. We have already noted that in Revelation 12:17 reference was made to those who "hold to the testimony (or witness) of Jesus." There is no doubt in my mind that the battle against the saints will increase. In fact, in Daniel 7 we see that the one who will "make alterations in times and law", and who will speak out against the Most High will also seek to "wear down the saints of the Highest One." The time of his operation is limited, it seems, to three and a half years (Daniel 7:25), and for that we can be most grateful. Nevertheless, that time will be intense.

While I have already mentioned the apostasy (a falling away), part of that is linked to deception as we see from 1 Timothy 4:1. They will fall away because they pay attention to deceitful spirits (AV: seducing spirits – literally, spirits which lead astray) and doctrines of demons.

Do not think that it will necessarily be blatantly obvious although in some cases it may be so. Evolution is a denial of God as Creator, and removes not only the concept of God creating all things, but also that He, therefore, has a right to determine our conduct. In the past, various doctrines have been put forward undermining the divinity (or humanity) of Christ. Gnosticism at the end of the first century had a damnable effect upon the Church. The whole matter of sacraments being the chief means of salvation undermines any assurance of salvation. Transubstantiation (the supposed transformation of bread and wine in to literal blood) with Christ having to be offered up again through the mass as part of the work of salvation, is again error and is, in effect, sheer blasphemy.

The teaching on the atonement by those within the Word of Faith movement is also blasphemous. They teach that the blood of Christ was not sufficient to atone, but that Christ had to descend into hell and take on a satanic nature and be born again. If Jesus had ever taken a satanic nature, then He would have needed salvation. This teaching came about through so-called special revelation, and on a misinterpretation that God made Jesus "to be sin for us . . ." (2 Corinthians 5:20). Without going into a great deal of detail, we should note that Scripture also states that "He knew no sin". They also say that when Jesus said, "It is finished" as He died upon the cross, He was stating that the Old Covenant was finished rather than that His work of bringing salvation was finished. Scripture is very clear that the blood of Christ was a propitiation for our sin (Romans 3:25). Scripture also makes it clear that it was by the death of Christ on the cross that our sins were forgiven (see 1 Peter 3:18). It is also evident from the letter to the Hebrews that by His death, He has obtained eternal redemption for mankind. By His sacrifice on the cross, He has obtained eternal redemption "once for all" (see Hebrews 7:27; 9:12 and 10:10).

Who is to say what other demonic distortions will be taught in the coming days? These are blatant errors for those who are aware of such teachings, but people are not always aware of these false doctrines. However, there will be far more subtle approaches by Satan because, as Paul reminds us, the Devil is able to disguise Himself as an angel of light (2 Corinthians 11:14). In a sense, he did that with Eve by promising that she would be like God, knowing good and evil. He always plays upon our pride with his flattery.

I mentioned earlier the so-called Toronto blessing. Clearly, there were those who wanted to experience more of the Lord, but if they examined where it all began, they would have seen that it started with those who were in the Word of Faith movement with the false doctrine on the atonement. That in itself was a clear warning that we should be cautious. The so-called manifestations were not manifestations of the Spirit, for so much of what they claimed could never be authenticated from the Scriptures as being of God. Seducing spirits, leading astray the people of God, will be active in the last days.

Before leaving the matter of Toronto, I would like to quote from Aeron Morgan's book, *The Biblical Testing of Teachings and Manifestations*. He deals with the defence that some have made regarding the so-called manifestations of Toronto with that of the Welsh Revival. He states that no comparisons can be made to justify

> the strange phenomenon in such as the "Toronto" style meetings, where those who were invited to testify were seemingly unable to speak, or became incoherent, even losing their power to think, as they frustratingly sought to tell forth what they had intended to share. How pathetic it was to see men and women in what appeared to be a hypnotic state struggling to communicate their message or testimony, and how dishonouring to the Almighty when the congregation found it all an amusing spectacle and a "laughing" matter.
>
> It seems that in the so-called "new wave" meetings it is reported that men lose all consciousness of where they are and what they are doing. While there is a "sort" of preaching that takes place, much of which is extemporaneous, hence quite verbose but lacking in content, the true exposition of the Word of God is noticeably absent from these meetings. The so-called preaching of these preachers is pathetically void of sound Biblical content. In the Welsh Revival it was *so* different. In fact, R B Jones says that . . . "there was an intense hunger for the Word, and the awakened ones could not tolerate anything but the Word" (p. 196).

Another area of concern is that of false prophecies. I do believe in the gift of prophecy, but there have been so many false prophecies given and accepted by the Church. I am always very suspicious of extravagant and exaggerated promises of future blessing, especially if there is no word of caution, because most of God's promises are conditional.

At the time of Princess Diana's death, there was a prophecy that before the flowers could be removed from the streets, just as quickly revival would come to the nation. The woman who brought the prophecy had previously been shown that flowers would be piled up in the street as a result of a person's death. She thought that it might the Queen Mother who was going to die. When Diana died, however, she thought it must refer to her. Then she claims that she received the second part, namely the prophecy that revival would come before the flowers were removed. It is a warning to us that just because part seems to be right it does not mean that the whole thing is of God. Satan or our own hearts and minds can deceive us. The false prophets in Jeremiah's day were charged with speaking "a vision of their own imagination" (Jeremiah 23:16).

We, within the leadership of Intercessors For Britain, never believed the so-called prophecy above was a word from God. We also found ourselves challenging a word given by Paul Cain that revival was going to come in October 1990. There was no witness in our hearts and, in any case, why should God give a specific date? Paul Cain often brought prophecies linked with so-called signs – events that would prove the prophecy, but he has been proved to be a false prophet. In 2004, Paul Cain was disciplined by his church for alcoholism and homo-sexuality.

Again, it is worth noting that his teaching was false. He stated that a "super breed" of Christians would be produced before the return of Christ. I heard also his pastor, Mike Bickle, state that they believed seventy "super" apostles would go forth from their church and accomplish more than the early apostles. That does not tie in with the Scriptures which we have seen relating to the return of Christ. Just because prophecies seem to have some miraculous element, it does not mean they are right.

Jesus warned that there will be false signs and wonders in the last days, as well as false prophets. It is important that we recognise this fact lest we should be deceived. Again that was part of the trouble with the Toronto experience because people saw unusual phenomena they assumed it must be of God. Some of it we believe was carnal, but some came about as a result of deceiving spirits.

Paul, in speaking about the man of lawlessness being revealed, states that he will come "with the activity of Satan, with all power and signs and false wonders, and with all the deception of wickedness . . ." (2 Thessalonians 2:9, 10). The Book of Revelation (13:13) even shows that the false prophet (who accompanies the antichrist) will call down fire from heaven (just as Elijah did on Mount Carmel) and that he would "deceive those who dwell on the earth because of the signs . . ." (v. 14).

The third area of conflict is that of Satan acting as usurper in trying to gain a kingdom for himself. This will be the final battle which will undoubtedly have a military component (Armageddon) but also a spiritual one. I do not doubt for one moment that where it speaks of incense being added to the prayers of the saints in Revelation 8:4, it concerns those final days when believers will cry to God to be delivered from the lawless one. I wonder whether that "incense" which is added to the prayers of the saints isn't even the intercession of the Lord Himself, as He pleads on our behalf. Prayer surely will be a major part of that final battle as His saints "cry to Him day and night . . ." (Luke 18:7). He will vindicate His elect, for there is not the slightest reluctance to come to our aid, for He is not like the unjust judge.

Jesus will "slay" the lawless one "with the breath of His mouth" when He returns to earth (2 Thessalonians 2:8). We see so clearly the power of Jesus that He merely has to blow upon the antichrist and he is destroyed.

Although Christ's victory is assured, we need to understand that there will be difficult days which the saints will have to endure. We have already noticed that antichrist will make war against the saints and try to "wear out the saints of the Highest One . . ." Those who refuse to take the mark of the beast will not be able to trade, but I am sure that God is able to provide for His saints even as He did for Elijah.

There has been much speculation about what the mark of the beast will be. People become alarmed about bar codes on various products, microchips inserted in the forehead etc. No doubt modern technology will assist the antichrist in his ban against the saints, but we must not lose sight of the fact that the Book of Revelation links worship of the beast (antichrist) with the mark of the beast. That mark upon the forehead marks ownership and submission to Satan. I do not think the speculation helps, for we are in danger of missing the real point, and that is the mark involves being a devotee of antichrist, not that somehow we might be in danger innocently of taking the mark of the beast through some technological advance.

The Book of Revelation and Daniel both show that the antichrist will share his reign with ten other "kings". Some have linked this with ten leaders in the European Union, and it may yet turn out to be the case. Others have given evidence of plans to divide up the world into ten regions. That also is a very real possibility. What is clear from Daniel is that the fourth beast out of which comes the supremacy of antichrist is linked with the old Roman Empire, and that the nations will become subject to him (see Revelation 13:7). There is a Roman dimension to his kingdom, but a global aspect as well.

We have often prayed, in Intercessors For Britain, that we might be delivered from the European Union. Some might say, well if all the nations are to be controlled by antichrist how can the United Kingdom maintain something of its sovereignty? That is a very good question.

Within the Roman Empire, there were parts which were only partially under its control, meeting real resistance. I also notice that in spite of Antiochus Epiphanes dominating Israel and desecrating the temple, the Maccabees rose up in revolt, and largely threw off the yoke of that tyrant. It is worth remembering that Daniel in prophesying about these events speaks of such a resistance by saying, "the people who know their God will display strength and take action" (11:32). Over the years, as we have cried to God to be delivered from Europe (which we sense will be the power-base of antichrist), we have seen euroscepticism increase in our nation. If nothing else, it may give us just a little more time and freedom to openly proclaim the gospel – although even now it is becoming increasingly difficult under the Blair Government to proclaim Jesus as the only way of salvation.

Daniel also shows that in spite of the antichrist's attempts to wear down the saints, the court of Heaven will finally meet and "his [antichrist's] dominion will be taken away, annihilated and destroyed forever" (7:26). As John sees in his revelation, Babylon will be destroyed, and there will be a time when heaven will declare: "The kingdom of the world has become the kingdom of our Lord and His Christ, and He will reign forever and ever" (11:15). Daniel equally understands that "His [Jesus'] kingdom will be an everlasting kingdom, and all the dominions will serve and obey Him" (7:27).

The battle will be intense, but short-lived. Satan with his "anointed one" (antichrist) will control the world for a limited time – a period of three and a half years according to Daniel 7:25; 12:7 and Revelation 13:5. We need to understand that God's victory is assured, in order that we might live in the light of that coming victory of our returning King. In the meantime, we will need to be among those who pray, wrestling against principalities and powers. We need to pray that people will be saved right up to the end. We need also to "be on the alert with all perseverance and petition for all the saints" (Ephesians 6:18), for Satan will seek to put many out of the fight. "Be dressed in readiness, and keep your lamps lit" said Jesus (Luke 12:35).

CHAPTER SIX

JUDGEMENT OF THE NATIONS

God has always judged the nations, but as the days draw near to a final conclusion, I believe that some of the events which take place will be God's judgement on nations and leaders who oppose the will of God. Part of the final shaking, will be a shaking of the demonic powers behind those nations. Islam will receive a shaking as we have already shown. Therefore those Islamic nations will be brought low.

In our lifetime, we have seen the Berlin Wall fall, the Iron Curtain of Communism come down (although aspects of it still remain) and the British Empire collapse. Some of those events have concerned the nations' dealings with Israel. Britain did not hold to the Balfour Declaration but gave away what is now known as Jordan. All the territory which comprises modern day Israel, the Palestinian Authority and Jordan was originally declared to be a homeland for the Jews. Yet at the end of the Second World War, we were sending the Jews back to some of the same concentration camps from which they had come, or interning them in Cyprus instead of allowing them to enter their homeland. Little wonder that from that point on our Empire fell.

Germany was divided as a result of losing the war, but I believe its division was directly related to its treatment of Jews and the so-called "final solution" of extermination. It was only after a major Christian gathering, inaugurated by Intercessors For Germany, when they confessed Germany's sin, that reunification took place.

Let any nation that hinders the purposes of God concerning the return of the Jews be careful. They will know of God's judgement just as Pharaoh did when he tried to prevent the Israelites leaving Egypt. It may not be so dramatic, but it will be as sure.

Let not the Church either be arrogant in its dealing with the Jews. In Romans 11:20, 21, when Paul speaks about the ultimate salvation of Israel, he also warns the gentile Church: "Do not be conceited, but fear; for if God did not spare the natural branches, He will not spare you, either." Peter also reminds us that judgement begins with the household of God (1 Peter 4:17). If the Church begins to oppose the purposes of God regarding Israel, then it too will know the opposition of the Lord just as surely as Haman, Balaam and Egypt did.

In this matter of God's judgement, we need to consider the matter of what many might call natural disasters. In Scripture, war, famine and earthquakes are often shown to be the judgement of God. Therefore, if there is an increase in these events towards the end times, are we to understand them as judgements of God? In many cases, I think we are to assume that is the case. In some instances, God may be trying to get our attention so that we call upon Him in our distress. Many have found God as a result of some personal crisis. God may, therefore, cause a time of shaking that He might bring people into His eternal Kingdom. Even in the midst of judgement His ultimate aim is to save men and women from a greater disaster, namely eternal judgement.

Isaiah understood that God's judgement was often redemptive. He speaks of observing God's judgements as he longs for the memory of God's name to be rekindled. Then he adds, in Isaiah 26:9, 10, "At night my soul longs for You, indeed, my spirit within me seeks You diligently; for when the earth experiences Your judgements the inhabitants of the world learn righteousness. Though the wicked is shown favour, he does not learn righteousness; he deals unjustly in the land of uprightness, and does not perceive the majesty of the Lord." Like any child who misbehaves, there are times when mankind needs to be brought up sharply so as to consider his or her behaviour. Only then will we learn.

There are also situations when God's judgement is a matter of taking away the restraint that He might otherwise impose. Scripture speaks of God giving people over to their own ways. In Psalm 81:11 we read: "But My people did not listen to My voice, and Israel did not obey Me. So I gave them over to the stubbornness of their heart, to walk in their own devices." Sometimes, we only learn from our own mistakes as we see the folly of our choices. Such judgements are to bring us to our senses.

Romans 1:18f would indicate a similar process. It speaks of the wrath of God being visited upon a people because they "suppress the truth in unrighteousness" even ignoring the evidence of God through His creation – something evolutionists do. Three times it states that "God gave them over . . .", first to permissiveness, then homosexuality, then to a depraved mind (vv. 24, 26 and 28). Our nation has been progressing down this slippery slope since the 1950s. In spite of sexually transmitted diseases being at almost epidemic proportions, we do not seem to have woken up to the fact that God's restrictions on sexual activity are for our well-being, not because He is a killjoy.

There are, however, times when a situation becomes so bad that God has no option, but to remove the wicked completely. Although He has since stated that He would never again destroy the world by flood, it is clear that in Noah's time the world had become so wicked that God had no alternative but to destroy the world. The situation had become so evil in Sodom and Gomorrah that God was forced to act, although even there He rescued Lot, his wife (temporarily) and his daughters. Israel went into exile because of its rebellion against the Most High God.

I believe that our nation has already experienced a number of judgements, including the hurricane sweeping across the southeast; the fire at York Minster; BSE, and foot and mouth disease. There have been train disasters, some of which have had uncanny events leading up to the crash. We have to recognise the truth of Amos' words when he wrote: "If a calamity occurs in a city has not the Lord done it?" (v. 6). Later, the prophet brings a message from God that although various disasters have overtaken them, including famine, drought, scorching wind, mildew, caterpillars and even war, "Yet you have not returned to Me, declares the Lord" (vv. 6, 8, 9, 10, 11).

The difficulty, sometimes, is knowing when God is just trying to get our attention or when it is a more serious matter. The earthquake and tsunami on Boxing Day 2004 and Hurricane Katrina (just to name two) were more than just natural disasters. God is not overwhelmed by natural causes, for He holds all creation under His control. Indeed the Psalmist understood that "The LORD sat as King at the flood; yes, the LORD sits as King forever" (Psalm 29:10).

I find it significant that the previous year (Boxing Day 2003), the Iranian city of Bam was rocked by an earthquake. Is the date a mere coincidence? The fact is that the epicentre of both earthquakes took place in Muslim countries. Those countries which were affected by the Tsunami were all idolatrous nations, and they have all persecuted Christians and opposed Christianity from Indonesia in the East to Sudan in the West. Some of those nations have been involved in paedophilia, temple prostitution and other degrading practices. While some Christians may have perished, there have been remarkable stories of many believers escaping death and disaster.

Yet, we need to be careful in pointing the finger of blame. Jesus was once asked about disasters which had fallen on Israel such as a massacre of Jews, by Roman soldiers, at a religious festival, or the collapse of a tower with a number of deaths. His reply was simply that they were not more wicked than the rest of the people, "but unless you repent, you will all likewise perish" (Luke 13:3, 5). Interestingly, Jesus had been speaking about the fact that people could recognise indications of what the weather would be like, but they could not understand the signs of the times. For them, Jesus was indicating that judgement and destruction lay ahead of them as a nation if they did not repent. In AD 70 Jerusalem and the temple they so prized were destroyed. It would seem that the earlier disasters were a warning of a greater disaster to follow, if they did not repent. We have been warned as a nation, but the warnings have largely gone unheeded.

We might reflect on the plagues of Egypt. They began in a relatively minor way, growing in greater severity. Their crops and cattle were affected, but finally human life was touched. It is as a last resort that God brings death upon a nation. God made it plain that He would strike down the firstborn of the Egyptians – they had sought to kill *every* male Israelite child – stating that He was executing not only His judgement upon Egypt, but also upon "the gods of Egypt" (Exodus 12:12).

Some of God's judgements are as much upon the false gods, idols and demonic powers, as against the people. God seeks to demonstrate that the gods are powerless to help the people in order that they might instead turn to Him for salvation. "There is no other name under heaven that has been given among men by which we must be saved" (Acts 4:12) – only the name of Jesus. He Himself said, "No one comes to the Father but through Me" (John 14:6). The shaking of those idol thrones and demonic strongholds is to demonstrate that they are powerless to save.

The Book of Revelation shows various catastrophes coming upon the world such as plagues, earthquakes, famines and wars. It is a time of tribulation, but also judgement. It is a matter of shaking the world from its complacency to seek salvation from God, but undoubtedly that time is also a matter of judging the nations.

Amos poses an interesting question when he writes: "Alas, you who are longing for the day of the Lord, for what purpose will the day of the Lord be to you?" (Amos 5:18). We think of the day of the Lord as the day Jesus returns, but again we must remember the run-up to His return is when the powers in the heavens are shaken. His judgement will be upon those powers of darkness and, of course, it will usher in the final judgement for all mankind. Rightly, therefore, does Amos pose the question and then adds: "It will be darkness and not light; as when a man flees from a lion and a bear meets him, or he goes home, leans his hand against the wall and a snake bites him. Will not the day of the Lord be darkness instead of light, even gloom, with no brightness in it?" (Amos 5:18–20).

Ezekiel gives a similar warning: "For the day is near, even the day of the Lord is near; it will be a day of clouds, a time of doom for the nations" (Ezekiel 30:3). While there are many days of the Lord when He judges nations, there is one ultimate day of the Lord.

Isaiah also sees that day coming for he writes: "Wail, for the day of the Lord is near! It will come as destruction from the Almighty . . . Behold the day of the Lord is coming, cruel, with fury and burning anger, to make the land a desolation; and He will exterminate its sinners from it. For the stars of heaven and their constellations will not flash forth their light; the sun will be dark when it rises and the moon will not shed its light. Thus I will punish the world for its evil and the wicked for their iniquity . . ." (Isaiah 13:6, 9–11). He utters similar words in chapters 24 and 26 stating that sun and moon will be affected. Jesus also gave a clear indication that this would happen immediately before His return. Therefore, we can see that there is a period of shaking and judgement coming upon the nations before His return.

I return to the starting point in this chapter; that of Israel. In Joel 3, we find a scenario that is portrayed regarding Israel coming under attack from the surrounding nations. I have no doubt that will occur in the future. It contains the verse (14), "Multitudes, multitudes in the valley of decision! For the day of the Lord is near in the valley of decision." It is amazing how often this is interpreted as people coming to salvation and as evidence of an end-time revival. The valley mentioned is "the valley of Jehoshaphat, for there I will sit to judge the nations." Jehoshaphat means "the Lord judges". It speaks, too, of the winepress being full "for their wickedness is great" (vv. 12, 13). This has nothing to do with revival, but has everything to do with judgement. The winepress with "the blood" (red colouring) of grapes speaks of bloodshed in battle as the Lord intervenes on behalf of Israel. Let the nations beware that they rise or fall on their attitude to Israel. Equally, let mankind understand that iniquity will not go unpunished. We may be judged in this world in various ways if we do not repent, but we shall certainly be judged in the next if we do not repent and believe on the Lord Jesus as Saviour and Lord.

In Revelation 9, it talks about various judgements that are to come upon the earth, but it states, in the last verse, that "they did not repent of their murders nor of their sorceries nor of their immorality nor of their thefts." God was seeking to bring about repentance, but they failed to respond. It seems to me there comes a point that all who will repent and call upon the name of the Lord will have done so. However, the judgements of God are to bring them to repentance, before the final judgement when they can no longer repent but will be sentenced for their sin. They will have chosen to live without God, and they will spend eternity away from the presence of God. That is Hell!

CHAPTER SEVEN

TRIBULATION OR RAPTURE?

There is a great deal of debate between evangelicals as to whether the Church will be raptured before the tribulation. Before we deal with that matter, we may need to clarify the word "rapture". It is not a biblical word, but it refers to believers ascending to meet the Lord in the air at His return.

Some also want to make a division between the appearing of the Lord to the Church, when they will meet him in the air as 1 Thessalonians 4:16f shows, and His return to earth. Some say that it is between these two events, His appearing and His return, that the Jews as a nation are saved. They also state that as the Church has been raptured at this point, then the Holy Spirit is removed from the world. If that is the case, then how can the Jews be born again by the Spirit?

What is more, however, Paul, in 2 Thessalonians 2:1–6, speaks of "the coming of our Lord Jesus Christ and our gathering to Him" (v. 1). That is the reverse order as some would see it, for they see our gathering to Him, and then His coming.

Scripture seems to put the two together as part of the same event.

When Paul writes in verse 6: ". . . you know what restrains him now, so that in his time he will be revealed", some Christians believe that it is the Holy Spirit who restrains the mystery of lawlessness and the coming of the lawless one. Yet the lawless one is revealed *before* the Church is caught up to meet the Lord. The restraint is taken away before we are gathered to the Lord. Paul clearly states, concerning the coming of the Lord and our gathering to Him that this will not come "unless the apostasy (falling away) comes first, and the man of lawlessness is revealed, the son of destruction, who opposes and exalts himself above every so-called god or object of worship . . ." The man of lawlessness will be seen before we are "raptured". Therefore it cannot be the Holy Spirit who is the restraining influence, for if the Church is still here at that point, the Holy Spirit must be. It is much more likely to be an angel that is restraining the mystery of lawlessness as is seen in the Book of Revelation where angels release things, but also bind Satan.

As I commented previously, we felt that a real measure of restraint against lawlessness was removed when Tony Blair won the election in 1997. Certainly ungodly legislation followed and there was a real change in the spiritual and moral climate of our nation. That is likely to happen on a larger scale preceding the appearance of the man of lawlessness.

Part of the argument for saying that the Church will be raptured before the return of Christ is that some see the tribulation as God's judgement or wrath upon an unbelieving world; but is that a correct consideration of the subject?

The Greek word (*thlipsis*) which is often translated "tribulation" means "distress, affliction, pressure, trial". It comes from a verb (*thlibo*) which means "to squeeze, press, afflict" and it is used in a passive form to mean "narrow" such as in Matthew 7:14. The narrow way is one where we are "pressed in" or constrained to walk God's way rather than the broad way of the world. It is not surprising, therefore, that Jesus said, "In the world you will have tribulation, but take courage; I have overcome the world" (John 16:33).

The apostle Paul stated: "through many tribulations we must enter the Kingdom of God" (Acts 14:22). Paul clearly knew that from experience, for just prior to making this statement, he had been stoned at Derbe and left for dead! In writing to the Church at Thessalonica he wrote that they had "received the word in much tribulation with joy in the Holy Spirit" (1 Thessalonians 1:6). The Church there had been born in the midst of persecution.

Paul, in writing to the Romans, asked the question: "Who will separate us from the love of Christ? Will tribulation (*thlipsis*), or distress, or persecution, or famine, or nakedness, or peril, or sword? Just as it is written, for Your sake we are being put to death all day long . . ." (Romans 8:36). The way of the Christian is one where we are constantly facing tribulation in one form or another, so why should we be exempt from what is often referred to as "*the* tribulation"?

The tribulation is seen by many as being particularly related to the Jews. Indeed, as we have seen, some would maintain that the Church will be raptured before the tribulation and that it is the Jews and Israel which will experience such a time of trouble, resulting eventually in their salvation. There certainly is an element of truth in this. It is while Jesus is speaking about the destruction of the temple that He later mentions the tribulation (Mark 13, Matthew 24 and Luke 21). He is asked about its destruction and the events leading up to the end. While Jesus may begin by talking about events that take place in AD 70, he quickly moves on to talk about world events which would take place before His return. There would be famines and earthquakes in various places, and that "the gospel would be preached in the whole world as a testimony to all the nations, and then the end will come" (Matthew 24:14). In other words it is not just about situations concerning Israel, but the whole world.

In Jeremiah 30:7 it speaks of "the time of Jacob's distress" but in the passage it also speaks of the New Covenant made with Israel when "they will all know the Lord." Clearly the New Covenant was initiated through the death of the Messiah, but they, as a nation, have not yet entered into that place where they will all know the Lord. The time of distress (tribulation) will cause them to call upon the Lord. Zechariah 12 points to a time when Jerusalem becomes "a heavy stone for all the peoples" and all the nations will attack Israel. God then pours out "the Spirit of grace and supplication" leading to repentance and recognition of their Messiah.

We should also note that in Revelation 7, 144,000 are sealed so that no harm can fall upon them. There are 12,000 from every tribe of Israel. These are clearly symbolic numbers where the number twelve reminds us of God's chosen people (twelve tribes, twelve apostles). Therefore, we see that God intends to protect (those who are sealed) thousands of Jews from all the tribes from those things that are coming upon the earth. The chapter speaks too of those who have come out of the great tribulation. If this refers to *the* tribulation (as against many other times of distress), then we need to note that the previous chapter speaks of suffering coming upon the whole earth. It is not just a time of trouble for Jews only, but the whole world. The events which follow in the next chapters of Revelation are also events which the whole earth experiences and not just Israel.

To return again to the situation which Jesus covers concerning the tribulation, He talks about signs in the sun, moon and stars, "and on the earth dismay among the nations, in perplexity at the roaring of the sea and the waves, men fainting from fear . . ." Jesus then says, in Luke 21:25, 28 as we have seen, "when these things begin to take place, straighten up and lift up your heads, because your redemption (i.e. being set free from these things) draws near."

In Matthew's gospel, Jesus warns that there will be a great tribulation (time of distress) such as had never been seen before and that "unless those days had been cut short, no life would have been saved; but for the sake of the *elect* those days will be cut short" (24:22). He then states that "immediately after the tribulation" the moon, stars and the powers in the heavens will be shaken, then the Son of Man will come on the clouds of heaven in "power and great glory" and the angels "will gather together His *elect* from the four winds, from one end of the sky to the other" (vv. 29–31). It would seem from this that our gathering to Him takes place after the tribulation.

Some, however, would say that as Jesus is talking to the disciples about Jewish events – the destruction of the temple – He is talking about a Jewish elect who are saved during this time, and are then gathered to the Lord. In response to that, we need to say that all Christ's teaching was given to the disciples (Jews). It would be foolish, therefore, to say that His teaching has no relevance for a gentile church as far as the end times are concerned.

Secondly, we have already seen that Jesus is not simply talking about Jewish events, but world events. He talks about the destruction of all life unless that time of tribulation is shortened, but for the sake of the elect those days would be cut short. Clearly, Jesus is talking here about the possibility of total annihilation, therefore the context implies that the word "elect" refers to believers worldwide and not simply to Jews.

Jesus also talks about the "elect" being gathered from the four corners of the earth. Some say that this refers to the Jews who have been scattered around the globe, but Ezekiel 36 speaks of the Jews being restored to their land, and then God will wash them with clean water and give them a new heart and put His Spirit in them. Therefore, the Jews are no longer scattered across the globe. It would seem that His elect who are gathered from the four quarters are believers in the Lord Jesus Christ, Jew and gentile together. In any case, the word "elect" in Scripture is used of all God's chosen ones – Jewish and gentile believers in Jesus.

There is a further consideration as to whether the Jews have a further opportunity to be saved after the Church has been raptured. Peter clearly sees no difference between Jew and Gentile, but rather sees the day of grace running out with the return of the Lord. Speaking of "the promise of His coming", he adds, "The Lord is not slow about His promise, as some count slowness, but is patient toward you, not wishing for any to perish but for all to come to repentance" (2 Peter 3:4 and 9). Obviously, Peter considers that with the return of Jesus, the time for repentance and salvation has come to an end. Surely the whole world is dealt with on the same basis. Neither Jesus, nor Peter, nor Paul give any indication that God has a different timetable for the Jews than for gentiles. In the parable of the ten virgins, in Matthew 25, when the midnight cry goes up that the bridegroom has come, then the door closes. To those outside, Jesus will reply, "Truly I say to you, I do not know you." He then adds: "Be on the alert then, for you do not know the day nor the hour [of His coming]."

It would seem, therefore, that the Church will go through at least part of the tribulation before the return of Christ. Again, I respect the fact that others will take a different view to me, but I would rather warn that we will face a time of distress as believers and be wrong, than say we will be raptured before the tribulation and find that we have to face it. It is better to be prepared for the worst than to be caught totally unprepared and ill-equipped to face such a time of distress.

It is my belief that many prefer to believe in a pre-tribulation rapture (i.e. Jesus will come for His Church before the tribulation), because it is more comforting. I believe, however, that in many ways the greatest opportunity for sharing the gospel is in times of distress. As believers, we can face the world's disasters and difficulties with a composure and radiance just because we know what our final destiny is. We have an unshakeable kingdom! We have a glorious inheritance which the world cannot take away. What is more we have the grace of God to face all that may come our way. When Paul was facing a period in his life in which he experienced weaknesses, insults, distresses, persecutions and difficulties (an attack of an evil spirit – Paul's thorn in the flesh),

he proved the truth of the Lord's words: "My grace is sufficient for you, for power is perfected in weakness."

The tribulation seems to me to be a time of distress which the
world will experience: it is not primarily connected with judgement or the wrath of God upon a rebellious world. Its purpose
may well be to cause men and women to cry out to God for salvation while there is time! It would fit in with the whole concept
of God shaking the earth and the heavens once again, including
shaking the powers which are in the heavens which concludes
the period of tribulation (Mark 13:24 and Hebrew 12:26).

There does seem, however, to be a time of wrath which the
world does face. If we look at Revelation 14:14–20 we have
two situations. First of all we see (in verses 14–16) "one like the
Son of Man" seated, no longer on the throne, but on a white
cloud, and about to reap a harvest which "is ripe". Many see
this as an end-time revival, but that is to miss the significance
of "one like the Son of Man" (which is the very description
used of Jesus in Revelation 1:13) sitting on the cloud. Surely
this indicates that He is about to return for He will come on
the clouds of heaven, according Matthew 24:30. Also in the
parable of the tares (Matthew 13) Jesus shows that at the end
of the age, He will send out the reapers (His angels) and will
gather the wheat (believers) into His barn ("in the Kingdom of
His Father"). It is worthy of note that Jesus also says in that
parable, "first gather up the tares . . ." (v. 30). It seems to me
that is exactly what happens, for antichrist comes first to gather
together those who are his, giving them the mark of the beast.
Then Jesus sends forth His angels to gather the elect into His
"barn" or Kingdom. The "harvest" in Revelation 14:14f is that
of the saints being gathered into His barn – our eternal home.

In Revelation 14:17–20, we see that after the elect are gathered together, there is reference to grapes being gathered and thrown into "the great wine press of the wrath of God." Again, it seems to me that although the Church will experience the tribulation, it will not experience the great wrath of God for we shall have been gathered safely into His Kingdom. There may be a brief time – a time of wrath – between our being caught up in the air with the Lord, and then coming to reign with Him on earth.

Another indication as to the timing of the Lord's return may be given in Revelation 16:15. The event is the final world war which will take place on the earth, namely Armageddon. It is placed at the very time when the bowls of wrath are being poured out. At that point in the narrative the Lord testifies, "Behold, I am coming like a thief. Blessed is the one who stays awake and keeps his clothes, so that he will not walk about naked and men will not see his shame [i.e. having his sin exposed]" There seems to be here a clear reference to the fact that Jesus comes at this point, and that we need to maintain our witness and personal integrity.

We may differ as believers over these matters, for God may have partially veiled these things, so that we live in a constant state of being ready. At the same time, we must surely agree that He is coming again, and we need to be ready for His return. We need to get ready now for the New Jerusalem. I have a feeling that the situation which will take place before His return, such as the tribulation, will be a time when believers are refined by those events, so that we are ready for an eternal Kingdom where only righteousness dwells.

CHAPTER EIGHT

STANDING FIRM

There is no doubt that the final days, before the return of Christ, will be difficult for the believer. If we do experience the tribulation before the return of Christ, then it will be a difficult time for everyone, but a real opportunity for us to bear witness to Christ. We will be looking up with anticipation for the return of Jesus when other people's hearts will be failing them for fear. People will no doubt ask us why we are not depressed or afraid at the prevailing conditions. We can then refer to the words of Jesus regarding the end-times, showing them that it is not yet too late to respond to the grace of God.

Peter also reminds us that the prophetic word is like "a lamp shining in a dark place, until the day dawns and the morning star arises in your hearts" (2 Peter 1:19). The morning star heralds the dawn of a new day. The first evidence concerning the Day of Lord will be within our hearts. Day-by-day the assurance will increase that He is "right at the door" (see Matthew 14:33). The prophetic signs which are given in

God's Word, along with the inner witness of the Spirit, will convince us that His coming is imminent.

The awareness of His near return will be a source of encouragement during those difficult days. During the time that the antichrist is in control those who do not have "the mark of the beast" will not be able to trade. We do not know the full implications of this, but God is more than able to take care of the saints as he did for the Old Testament saints such as Elijah when he was fed by the ravens.

We need to explore this area a little further to gain understanding. First of all, what is the meaning of "the beast"? It is interesting that in Revelation 13 the beast is described as looking like a leopard, having feet like a bear, and a mouth like a lion. This is in reverse order to that which we find in Daniel 7. There they represent firstly the Babylonian Empire, then the Persian followed by the Greek, but the fourth beast which has ten horns represents the Roman Empire. These world empires can also be identified from Daniel 2 where King Nebuchadnezzar is shown the world powers which are to follow him, through Daniel's interpretation. We are told that in the time of the fourth (Roman) kingdom "the God of Heaven will set up a kingdom which will never be destroyed, and that kingdom will not be left for another people; it will crush and put an end to all these kingdoms, but it will itself endure forever" (Daniel 2:44). It was during the time of the Roman Empire that Jesus was born ushering in the Kingdom of God.

In Daniel 7, the third beast, or great world power, has four wings and four heads. We know that after the death of Alexander the Great, his Greek Empire, split into four sections.

This helps to confirm the order of the four world powers following each other: Babylonian, Persian, Greek and Roman. When Daniel seeks understanding about the fourth beast with its ten horns, he is told by God "out of this kingdom ten kings will arise; and another will arise after them. . . . He will speak out against the Most High and wear down the saints of the Highest One, and he will intend to make alterations in times and in law (*torah*, Hebrew meaning 'instruction')" for what appears to be three and half years. Finally his sovereignty is taken away and utterly destroyed, but then the sovereignty and dominion is given to the saints of the Highest One whose Kingdom is an everlasting Kingdom – to the Lord Jesus Christ Himself.

There is such a similarity between Daniel's account and the Book of Revelation that we cannot be in doubt that they are describing the same events. However, the beast described in Revelation 13 has similarities to the preceding beasts mentioned in Daniel 7. We must assume, therefore, that the beast in Revelation 13 which has ten horns is that of the Roman Empire, but has similar traits to those of the Babylonian, Persian and Greek Empires. They all sought to undermine the purposes of God and persecute the people of God. The beast in Revelation does exactly the same.

We might note, too, that what Nebuchanezzar saw as a beautiful statue (in Daniel 2), God revealed to Daniel that those world powers were ravenous beasts. Man in his arrogance marvels at the splendour of his achievements as Nebuchadnezzar did: "Is this not Babylon the great, which I myself have built as a royal residence by the might of my power and for the glory of my majesty?" (Daniel 4:30).

God, however, sees it exactly how it is: arrogant, wicked, and aggressively opposed to His purposes.

The beast in Revelation has another aspect which is not mentioned in Daniel. It states that the beast who had received a fatal wound makes an amazing recovery (13:3, 12, 14). It also describes the beast as one which "was, and is not, and is about to come up out of the abyss and go to destruction." It also states in the same verse that "he was and is not and will come."

If we are right in identifying this beast as the Roman Empire (and Daniel seems to make it abundantly clear), then the emergence of the European Union could be the revival of the Roman Empire. That is exactly what the Founding Fathers of the EU were seeking to do. The treaty of Rome was signed right in the heart of the ruins of ancient Rome. There have been many attempts to keep alive that ancient empire in the form of the Holy Roman Empire. Napoleon and Hitler also saw themselves as restoring the might of Rome, but the extent of the EU roughly replicates the Roman Empire although, as is mentioned in Daniel 2, its extremities did not adhere together just as clay and iron do not mix. If that was true of the old empire perhaps it might be true of today's version, perhaps even leaving Britain out on a limb. Let us pray that may be the case, although the time will come when antichrist will seek to dominate the whole world. We are fast moving towards a one world government.

To return to "the mark of the beast". It would seem from Revelation 14:9, 11 that the mark is given to those who worship the beast – the antichrist. There is all sorts of speculation about the nature of the mark; such as a microchip planted in the forehead and right hand. Modern technology could obviously be used for some global trade embargo against those who do not submit to the beast. Some, even now, will not use credit cards lest they inadvertently receive the mark; nevertheless we should recognise that the mark is given to those who worship the beast. It is such worshippers of the beast who receive his mark (clearly identifying them as belonging to him) and who are thrown into the lake of fire (Revelation 20:4).

There is another area which we ought to cover. Riding on the beast is a woman described as "Babylon the Great, the mother of harlots and of the abominations of the earth" (Revelation 17:5). Harlotry in Scripture has always been seen as a picture of idolatry and turning to false religion. Israel was charged with harlotry when she went after other gods.

The Hebrew word for Babylon is *Babel* which of course takes us back to the tower of Babel. Geographically it was situated in Mesopotamia, but spiritually it reminds us of the events surrounding its beginning. Mankind was seeking to build its way up to heaven, and in the process, seeking to bring security for itself and a reputation. That is the origin (mother) of every false religion. By one's own efforts, devotees of every religion seek to enter some sort of nirvana or heaven thus finding security for the soul, but it is not possible! Once man has sinned, then he stands condemned, for "the wages of sin is death" (Romans 6:23). We cannot reach up to heaven by our own efforts. It requires One to come down from Heaven, even the Son of God.

Babylon then is every false religious system which relies on "good works" (i.e. religious practices and socially acceptable good deeds). Babylon is described as the mother of harlots for the events at Babel have spawned a plethora of false religions.

Many of the Reformers saw Roman Catholicism as Babylon. In many ways, they were right. Catholicism is a syncretistic religion and therefore idolatrous. Let us take just one example. Mary is afforded a place in Catholic theology which finds no place in Scripture. She is referred to as "the Queen of Heaven". That title was given to Ishtar and is referred to by Jeremiah where the women, in particular, had offered up sacrifices to her. The New Testament, however, gives no such title to Mary, but it has been attributed to her by the traditions of the Roman Catholic Church. Intercession to the saints and Mary also finds no place in Scripture for we have One (Jesus) who ever lives to make intercession for us (see Hebrews 7:25).

Catholicism has distorted the gospel making it a matter of works. The catechism states that "the sacraments are the chief means of salvation", therefore attendance at mass becomes a means of gaining merit as does penance, indulgences and good works. It is classically Babylonian in emphasis.

In recent years, Catholicism has increasingly reached out to other religions and held interfaith events at Assisi (It is not so keen, however, to reach out to evangelicals). Almost certainly Babylon will have at its heart the Catholic Church, but at the same time a one world religious system will emerge. Even now the United Nations has proclaimed that the world's religions are of equal value, but God's Word makes it plain that Jesus is the only way to the Father, and that salvation lies in Him alone. The one world Babylonian system is emerging and liberal, apostate elements within the traditional denominations will move ever closer together. It is one reason why we, in Intercessors For Britain, are greatly concerned about churches together as truth is abandoned for a false unity.

This mysterious woman in Revelation rides on the back of the beast. The Roman Catholic Church seeks to control Europe, but it is interesting that in the proposed EU Constitution there was no reference to Europe's Christian background, as the Roman Catholic Church wanted.

However, we might note that the founding fathers of the EU, Alcide De Gasperi, Robert Schuman and Konrad Adenauer, have all been canonised by the Catholic Church for founding the Union on Roman Catholic principles. As early as 1952, in his Christmas broadcast, Pope Pius XII envisaged "a Christian order which alone is able to guarantee peace. To this goal the resources of the Church are now directed." Yet it was this same Pope who formed a Concordat with Hitler and Mussolini, and colluded with the Nazi Ustashi in Yugoslavia in slaughtering 240,000 Orthodox Serbs and forcibly converting over 750,000 to Roman Catholicism. In February 1952, he encouraged the faithful of Rome by saying, "The whole world must be rebuilt from its foundations." Pope John XXIII talked about a European religio-political system that would be "the greatest [Roman] Catholic superstate the world has ever known." Later the Papal Nuncio in Brussels described the EU as "a Catholic Confederation of States".

Malachi Martin, a former Jesuit priest at the heart of the Vatican wrote a book called *The Keys of This Blood* with the subtitle *Pope John Paul II versus Russia and the West for control of the New World Order*. Martin points out that with the Vatican's 116 embassies, institutions and priests around the world, it is in a position to influence the world, and that the Pope deliberately set himself the goal of establishing a high international profile which he certainly did by his many visits to so many countries. His death and funeral bore witness to his impact upon the world. Martin adds, however, "What captures the unwavering attention of the secular leaders of the world in this remarkable network of the Roman Catholic Church is precisely the fact that it places at the personal disposal of the Pope a supranational, supercontinental, supra-trade-bloc structure that is so built and orientated that if tomorrow or next week, by a sudden miracle, a one-world government were established, the Church would not have to undergo any essential change in order to retain its dominant position and to further its global aims" (pp. 142–3).

In the end, I feel that the woman riding on the beast in the Book of Revelation represents something of a one world religion, but strongly linked and controlled by the Roman Catholic Church, for mystery Babylon is that religious system where man tries to reach heaven by his own efforts. It began at Babel (Babylon), but it continues throughout the world's religions. According to the Book of Revelation the woman rides the beast, for a while, seeking to control the political system, but in the end, the beast turns on the woman and destroys her.

It will not be easy for the true believer to stand against the tide in those days to come. Indeed, at the time of Pope John Paul II's death and funeral service, it seemed that the world had been mesmerised by the papal events. Prime Ministers, presidents, princes, prelates and priests flocked to Rome to do homage to the dead Pope. It reminded me of the passage in Revelation which states: "All the nations have drunk of the wine of the passion of her immorality (false religion or idola-try), and the kings of the earth have committed acts of immorality (idolatry) with her . . ." I have never seen such idolising of a person in the whole of my lifetime – not even when Princess Diana died.

What will it be like when antichrist himself appears and "exalts himself above every so-called god or object of worship, displaying himself as being God"? (2 Thessalonians 2:4). I believe we caught a glimpse of what is to come in the eulogising of Pope John Paul II.

It will not be easy to resist the charisma of antichrist, espe-cially as he will be endowed with demonic power to produce false signs and wonders. Not everything supernatural is of God. There were those who fell for Toronto because they did not distinguish between what is of God, and what is of the flesh or the demonic. We must test the spirits to see whether they are of God (see 1 John 4:1f).

Yet in this greatest of battles with the enemy of our souls, we are able to stand firm. What encourages me is that in Ephesians 6:10–17 (the passage dealing with wrestling against principalities and powers), it states three times, "stand firm". In verse 13, we are told to "take up the full armour of God, so that you will be able to resist in the evil day, and having done everything to stand firm." If those final days of human history are going to be darkened by the wickedness of anti-christ and a diabolical religious system, we clearly can resist in the evil day and stand firm. We will need that armour to be intact. Our righteousness in Christ (the breastplate) will need to be maintained. We will need to surround our lives with the belt of truth to avoid deception. Our minds must be protected from the propaganda of the enemy. Faith in God and His Word (our shield) regarding the final outcome and the coming of the Lord will have to be uppermost in our thoughts. Even then we must metaphorically speaking have our boots on and be ready to share the gospel with others as opportunity arises. On the other hand, as has always been the case, we will need to be "as wise as serpents and harmless as doves" (Matthew 10:16).

However, the real clue to standing firm is found in verse 10 of Ephesians 6: "Be strong in the Lord and in the strength of His might." It is only in the strength which God gives that we can stand. Few have faced the onslaught of the enemy as Paul did when he was attacked in so many ways by "the messenger of Satan". God did not remove the attack, but gave grace so that he might be strong. If we examine all that the apostle experienced for the sake of the gospel (see 2 Corinthians 11:23–28) and see how he endured by the grace of God, then we shall be encouraged for the days that lie ahead.

Equally the writer to the Hebrews seeks to encourage the messianic believers by stating that they had need of endurance, giving a catalogue of Old Testament saints, in the eleventh chapter, who endured by faith. We should remember, too, that Jesus said, "the one who endures to the end, he will be saved" (Matthew 24:13).

In thinking about "the strength of His might", Paul uses a similar phrase in Ephesians 1 and reminds us that God's power towards us is measured in raising Christ from the dead and putting Him as head over all things, including principalities and powers, for the sake of the Church. In the third chapter, he shows us that we are strengthened in the inner man by the

Holy Spirit and by the incomprehensible love of God. Indeed, in Romans 8, Paul reminds us that nothing can separate us from the love of God and Christ, and that we are more than conquerors through Him who loved us. The mark of the believer is that he is an overcomer through Christ.

> Therefore, my beloved brethren, be steadfast, immovable, always abounding in the work of the Lord, knowing that your toil is not in vain in the Lord. (1 Corinthians 15:58)

CHAPTER NINE

GLOBAL GOVERNMENT

Having already touched on the matter of the beast and Babylon, I want to refer to another aspect of it. It is very clear that the antichrist will control the world. According to Revelation, he will have jurisdiction over the whole earth. Christians have been observing how everything is preparing the way for antichrist and his dominion.

In almost every area of life, we are seeing that everything is falling into place. In industry, we no longer deal with British firms, but our companies have been taken over by multinationals. It means that a nation can do very little regarding its own commerce because it is in the control of others who may live thousands of miles away. Power is increasingly passing into the hands of a few individuals. The turnover of Microsoft, the computer giant, is supposed to be greater than that of the United States of America. Our energy supplies and utilities rely increasingly on multinational companies and other nations. We can be held to ransom by those individuals or nations. We talk now about a global economy rather than the British economy.

There is very clear evidence that industrialists have played their part in moving us towards a one world government. Part of the plan to bring this about was to form economic trading blocks as Gary Kah explains in his book *En Route to Global Occupation*. He writes: ". . . it was soon realised that region-alized world government would be next to impossible to achieve politically because of resistance to the idea from the world's people. So the powers-that-be decided to divide the world into economic regions first, hoping to pave the way for later political unions based on these same geographical boundaries. In order to accomplish this feat, several special task organisations were established to oversee the creation of regional trade associations. The society responsible for Europe's economic integration would be the Bilderberg Group, better known as the Bilderbergers" (p. 38).

The group derived their name from the Bilderberg Hotel in Oosterbeek, Holland. According to Kah they were funded by major one-world institutions, including the Rockefeller and Ford Foundations with the express aim of "regionalising Europe". One of the leaders of the group, Giovanni Agnelli, the head of Fiat stated, "European integration is our goal and where the politicians have failed we industrialists hope to succeed" (quoted in *Newswatch* magazine March–April 1984).

The same article quoted George McGhee, the former US ambassador to West Germany as saying, "The Treaty of Rome which brought the Common Market into being was nurtured at the Bilderberg meetings." Of course, the "Common

Market", or the European Economic Community became known as the European Community and then the European Union. Its goal from the start was "ever closer union".

That of course was only part of the plan. Other sister organisations like the Council for Foreign Relations, the Club of Rome, the Trilateral Commission and the United Nations are all working towards one world government. It seems too that freemasonry has played a major part in this scheme. Certainly, there are close links between freemasonry and the Bilderbergers and also the Council for Foreign Relations. Freemasonry is clearly Luciferic (i.e. Satanic) in its upper echelons, so that it is playing its major part in forming the power base of the antichrist.

Increasingly the United Nations has been seen as the world's parliament. At one time, it would not intervene in a nation's internal policies, but that has changed considerably, especially since the first Gulf War after Iraq invaded Kuwait. Indeed, after that event George Bush (snr) spoke openly of the new world order. The UN has encouraged that new order of things. For instance, it has stated clearly that all religions are of equal value and should be respected as such. It also pushed for gay rights, as did the European Union.

Other groups such as the World Trade Organisation and G8 have also been pursuing global policies, so that national sovereignty is all the time being eroded. Nowhere is this erosion of sovereignty more obvious to us in Britain, than when we observe how much the European Union has control of the United Kingdom through treaties and regulations which emerge from Brussels. We find that the Westminster Parliament is often powerless to deal with various issues on a national basis because all laws and regulations are subject to those emanating from Brussels. Yet, only occasionally do our ministers admit that their hands are tied because the political elite of Europe seek to co-operate in forwarding their political aims of ever closer union.

Again, however, we can see that erosion of national sovereignty was part of the aim of the Bilderbergers. It can be seen in a quotation from Prince Bernhard of Holland (who was a principal owner of the Royal Dutch Shell Oil Company) when he wrote about the problems of advancing the aims of the Bilderbergers: ". . . the governments of the free nations are elected by the people, and if they do something the people don't like they are thrown out. It is difficult to re-educate the people who have been brought up on nationalism to the idea of relinquishing part of their sovereignty to a supranational body . . . This is the tragedy" (*En Route to Global Occupation*, p. 39).

Edward Heath deceived the British public when he stated that there would be no loss of British sovereignty in joining the EEC, although he did add that we would be pooling our sovereignty. The fact is we have lost almost entirely our sovereignty as a nation. We learnt much later that Ted Heath wanted to forward all the goals of ever closer union, including economic unity and the single currency. At the moment, we are still spared from the Euro and, therefore, we have at least a measure of control over our interest rates and some flexibility in economic policy.

However, to return to the original point: the EU is only part of the grand plan of bringing about one world government. The other organisations are playing their part in forwarding this cause. Other factors like the new age movement and multiculturalism are breaking down those barriers which once separated us. The environment and climate change are all being used as excuses to control nations and individuals in a way we have never seen before.

It is worth noting that the whole issue is being greatly distorted. In an article in the *Sunday Telegraph* (5 November 2006), Christopher Moncton accuses the UN and its scientists of distorting the truth. He reports how one person working on the subject of climate change was sent an email saying, "We have to get rid of the Medieval Warm Period." In the article, Christopher Monckton proceeded to state: "Scores of scientific papers show that the medieval warm period was real, global and up to 3°C warmer than now. Then, there were no glaciers in the tropical Andes: today they're there. There were Viking farms in Greenland: now they're under permafrost. There was little ice at the North Pole; a Chinese naval squadron sailed right around the Arctic in 1421 and found none.

"The Antarctic, which holds ninety per cent of the world's ice and nearly all its 160,000 glaciers, has cooled and gained ice-mass in the past 30 years, reversing a 6,000-year melting trend. Data from 6,000 boreholes worldwide show global temperatures were higher in the middle ages than now. And the snows of Kilimanjaro are vanishing not because summit temperature is rising (it isn't) but because post-colonial deforestation dried the air. Al Gore please note."

He continued, "In some places it was warmer in the Bronze Age and in Roman times. It wasn't CO_2 that caused those warm periods. It was the sun." According to Monckton, Sami

Solanki, a solar physicist, has said that in the past half-century the sun has been warmer than for many centuries.

National governments, The European Union and the United Nations are all playing upon the fears of climate change and global warming by distorting the facts – even exaggerating the amount by which sea levels are arising. As a result, we are all going to see increasing restrictions and regulations to control our lives. One thing is sure that through it all, we are seeing the advancement of global government leading to the appearance of Antichrist.

Another area which has helped globalism is that of a multi-faith agenda. Again, the United Nations has played a major part in promoting the ethos for a one world religion stating that all religions are of equal value. Our own government has done much to debunk Christianity and enhance the state of other religions. The multifaith culture is certainly advancing the development of "mystery Babylon" and the links that the harlot has with the beast as revealed in the Book of Revelation.

What God revealed to John all those centuries ago is being fulfilled in our day. The "political correctness" of Tony Blair's Government has eroded ethical standards set by God. It is interesting that Babylon is described as "the mother of harlots and of the abominations of the earth." Homosexuality is an abomination in the sight of God, and the Blair Government has done more than any other government to promote and protect the homosexual community. Equally, the Gender Recognition Act must be another abomination, for God clearly stipulated that a man should not wear women's clothing and vice versa (see Deuteronomy 22:5).

Although we see the development of the antichrist system, we need to remember that Jesus will destroy the Lawless One by "the breath of His mouth" at His return. The true Christ simply blows away the antichrist because God is putting every enemy under His feet.

In seeing the Harlot emerging – the false religious system linked with the Beast – we know that at the same time the Bride of Christ, the Church, will be preparing for the coming of the Bridegroom, Jesus. While we need to recognise what is happening in fulfilment of prophecy regarding one world government, we need to stay focused on what God is doing in bringing all things to a conclusion in Christ.

CHAPTER TEN

THE BRIDE IS PREPARED

Hallelujah! For Lord our God, the Almighty reigns. Let us rejoice and be glad and give the glory to Him, for the marriage of the Lamb has come and His bride has made herself ready. (Revelation 19:7)

There are those who see the Bride as representing a special section of the Church who are overcomers, but I find that difficult to comprehend as there seems to be little scriptural warrant for such a view, apart from a rather over-literal view of the parable of the ten virgins. In that parable, there are the five foolish and five wise virgins together with the bridegroom. There is, of course, no mention of a bride in the parable, but some would wish to force the interpretation and include a bride as well as the wedding guests, but that is to force the parable to unnecessary lengths. The parable is simply a warning to make sure we are ready for the return of Christ.

On the other hand, the basis for seeing the whole Church as the Bride of Christ begins in Ephesians 5. While there is no specific mention of the Church as being the Bride the implication is there. Paul is making a clear comparison between the relationship of husband and wife with that of Christ and the Church.

It talks of the husband being the head of the wife as Christ is head of the Church. In these days of the women's liberation movement, the concept of the husband's headship is contested and seen as old fashioned. Yet the headship of Christ over the Church is recognised as being right. Why do we accept the one and not the other? It is true that this idea of the husband's headship has been overdriven so that the husband often became, in Victorian circles, some sort of family tyrant. That concept has no basis in Scripture, for the husband has to love his wife as Christ "loved the Church and gave Himself up for her." While the wife may need to lay down her will in submitting to her husband, the husband needs to lay aside his self-will in the interests of the family. Above all, his love for his wife has to be a sacrificial love. A husband who loves his wife sacrificially, seeking to protect her, will not find any difficulty in his wife submitting to him.

While Paul is dealing with family matters here, for he goes on to speak about parent-child relationships, he, nevertheless, is instructing us, at the same time, about relationships between Christ and the Church. Indeed when he speaks about husband and wife being one flesh, he adds: "this mystery is great; but I am speaking with reference to Christ and the Church." The two relationships of husband and wife, and that of Christ and the Church are linked together for one illustrates the other.

It is fitting, therefore, to note the same passage speaks of Christ not only giving Himself up for the Church, but adds, "that He might sanctify her, having cleansed her by the washing of water with the word." The message of salvation through the death of Christ is what brings cleansing to our lives. Without the message of Christ's death on the cross together with repentance and faith on the part of the recipient, there can be no forgiveness and cleansing. The reference to water is not only a symbolism of washing away uncleanness, but also of baptism. The message to Paul by Ananias was, "Arise, and be baptised, and wash away your sins, calling on His name" (Acts 22:16). Peter uses similar imagery in 1 Peter 3:21. We might add here that in the New Testament, baptism always followed a profession of faith, and not the other way around.

Paul having, therefore, referred to the matter of "the washing of the water with the word" adds "that He might present to Himself the church in all her glory." I do not doubt for one moment that Paul is speaking of that future event when "the marriage of the Lamb" takes place "and His Bride has made herself ready." We should note too that the phrase "the marriage of the Lamb" reminds us that our future relationship with Christ is dependent on the fact that He is the sacrificial Lamb who took away our sin. In Revelation that event takes place after the destruction of Babylon. That, in itself, is significant, but the preparation obviously starts at conversion. It is there, by faith, we receive God's forgiveness and cleansing. Without the death of Christ and faith in Him, we cannot possibly be saved or be part of that fit partner for Him for eternity.

We are of course dealing with a metaphorical message in talking about being the Bride of Christ. I have seen, sometimes, some ladies take a rather sentimental and even dangerous view of Jesus being their personal Bridegroom. It is a corporate concept. The whole, redeemed Church of God throughout the ages is going to be the Bride. It is a reminder that the Church – not the world – has been chosen to be Christ's partner for eternity.

Actually, this is not simply a New Testament concept, for God said through Hosea: "I will betroth you to Me forever: yes, I will betroth you to Me in righteousness and in justice, in lovingkindness and in compassion, and I will betroth you to Me in faithfulness. Then you will know the Lord" (2:19, 20). This was in contrast to Hosea's unfaithful wife who played the harlot like Israel in turning to other gods. The time would come, when Israel would come to know the Lord and would truly be betrothed *for ever*. The redeemed of Israel, together with the gentile believers, will be betrothed and "married" for eternity.

Let me again, however, return to Ephesians, for Paul speaks of Christ "sanctifying her . . . that He might present to Himself the church in all her glory, having no spot or wrinkle or any such thing; but that she should be holy and blameless." That sanctifying process starts at conversion in each individual believer, but continues until He returns. The Holy Spirit goes on working in our lives until we are really ready to share eternity with Him. It seems to me that there is much refining before the Church reaches such a position.

It is one reason why I believe God will allow the antichrist to appear before the return of Christ. Those who are true believers in Christ, and are genuinely committed to serve Him as Lord, rather than just seeking God's blessing for themselves, will stand in that evil day. Again, we remind ourselves that Jesus stated that because lawlessness is increased, the love of many will grow cold. As we have already noted, lawlessness will increase leading up to the appearance of the Lawless One, and he will continue to make changes in law (*torah*) when he comes to the fore.

Peter speaks about facing various trials prior to the return of the Lord. In doing so, he states that those trials test the "genuineness" of our faith ("the proof of our faith") "even though tested by fire, may be found to result in praise and glory and honour at the revelation of Jesus Christ" (1 Peter 1:7). The context is clearly that of waiting for the Lord's return.

The matter of testing is something which is overlooked by many. James, also speaks of "various trials" declaring that such testing of our faith results in patience and the development of character. He goes on to state: "Blessed is the man who perseveres under trial; for once he has been approved (literally, "passed the test"), he will receive the crown of life which the Lord has promised to those who love Him" (see James 1:3, 4 and 10).

It is one reason why I am concerned that we do not make it too easy for unbelievers to come to Christ. Jesus tended to make it hard for followers to respond to Him. They were to deny themselves and take up their cross. Jesus pointed out that it would be costly to follow Him, and that they would face persecution. Some of the courses which are run for unbelievers seek to make it so attractive to become a Christian, and avoid the challenge of putting self to death, or even owning Christ as Lord as well as recognising Him as Saviour. Sadly, I believe that it will be amongst these that many will fall away when lawlessness is increased.

It is in that same context that Jesus talks about tribulation and enduring to the end. It is another reason why I am of the opinion that believers will have to go through the tribulation – or at least part of it. In that very context, Jesus reminds us that it is he who endures to the end who will be saved (Matthew 24:13). I believe it will be a time of preparation when the Bride will make herself ready.

In Revelation 19, the order of events is interesting. First of all Babylon is destroyed, then the "Marriage of the Lamb" takes place ("His Bride has made herself ready"), followed by the destruction of the beast and the armies who come to wage war against the Lord. Once again, we see that the Church is brought into conflict with the antichrist system. Indeed, the call goes out to the saints in the previous chapter to "come out of her, My people" in order to avoid being judged with her downfall. Once more the fettle of the saints will be tested as to whether they will separate themselves from the world's system. We might also remember, too, as this antichrist system develops, only those who worship the beast (antichrist) will be allowed to trade. Again, we can see that part of the preparation of the Bride is seen in being tested regarding faithfulness to Christ. Other suitors, as it were, are seeking the devotion of believers, but the true believer will have none of it, for their allegiance is to Christ and none other. We will not enter into some liaison with the harlot!

In 2 Corinthians 11:2 and 3, Paul states that he had sought to "betroth" the church in Corinth to Christ "as a pure virgin" but he was afraid that as Satan deceived Eve, the enemy would lead the Corinthians astray from "the simplicity and purity of devotion to Christ." What was happening to bring about this concern? False apostles had been influencing the church and "fleecing" them, by what appears to be a prosperity gospel. By way of contrast, Paul had sought to get nothing from the Corinthians so as not to be a burden to the young church.

He continues by saying that Satan can disguise himself "as an angel of light" and false apostles, therefore, "disguise themselves as servants of righteousness . . ." (see verses 13–15). We need to recognise that in subtle ways Satan comes, as he did to Eve by promising false things. In various ways, Satan will use people who seem to have a notable ministry, but subtly seeds are being sown which draw them further and further away from the Lord. I have seen such false apostles and prophets at work, filling people with pride and giving false promises which even end up ruining ministries, and certainly that pure devotion to Christ. Beware, Satan has many ways of diverting the Bride from getting ready for the return of the Lord and our eternal destiny.

Finally, it is worth remembering that any bride prepares herself for her wedding day. It is a special occasion! She will make sure that she is adequately prepared for the day. Having bathed herself, no doubt applying perfume, and having her hair styled, and her nails manicured, she then gives attention to the dress. Finally when she arrives at the church, with every detail in place, somebody will announce to the pastor "the bride is ready!" – and the ceremony begins.

What is all important is the white dress which symbolises purity. She has kept herself especially for her future husband. The bride of Christ is dressed in fine linen "bright and clean" which is "the righteous acts of the saints" (19:7). It is worth noting that the bridal gown is symbolic of the righteous lives which the saints have lived. Here is proof that the Bride actually consists of the saints of God, just as the Church does. Those comprising the true Church, however, will have sought to live righteously in preparation for life with Christ for eternity. Earthly desires will have grown dimmer and dimmer in preparation for the eternal home.

When I was preparing for the ministry, many of the fiancées of the students prepared themselves for their future life with their husbands, as secretaries or nurses. It was felt that such employment or vocation would equip them for the life ahead. I wonder whether the Church is giving as much attention to our future destiny.

In Philippians 3:14, Paul speaks about pressing "toward the goal for the prize of the upward call of God in Christ Jesus." He makes it clear that he has not yet become perfect, but that he is pressing forward. He ends the chapter by reminding the Philippians that they are citizens of heaven and that one day their bodies will be changed into conformity with Christ's glorious body. Paul's aim was to be ready to be a citizen of the New Jerusalem.

In Revelation 21, an angel offers to show John the Bride, the wife of the Lamb. When He sees the Bride it is nothing less than the New Jerusalem. We shall return to this matter later, but here is a clear reminder of our eternal destiny. The redeemed Church of God enters into a eternal relationship with Christ which supersedes anything on earth.

Engaged couples often have to spend part of their time in separate places. They have a close relationship, but it is carried on at a distance – at best a few streets away, but at worst perhaps even a continent away. Our relation with Christ has been somewhat distant, but the concept of the bride reminds us that we shall share eternity with Christ – and with God, the Father.

The Bride is the New Jerusalem! It is not two people living together in harmony, but the community of God living in a perfect world. Therefore, if the Bride is ready, then the Church will have come to the place where it has been refined by the Holy Spirit and by circumstances, to spend eternity in the presence of God, and His Son, and in community where nothing unclean will ever enter. Are you getting ready? In the words of John: "Beloved, now we are the children of God, and it has not appeared as yet what we will be. We know that when He appears, we will be like Him, because we will see Him just as He is. And everyone who has this hope fixed on Him purifies himself, just as He is pure" (1 John 3:3).

CHAPTER ELEVEN

REWARDED AND REIGNING

Part of being ready for His return is not simply being ready to be a good citizen of the New Jerusalem, but ready for further responsibilities. The idea of seeking rewards is not exactly free of self interest, but it does find a place in Scripture. While we would not want to base hard facts about the future on a parable, the fact is that in the parable of the talents, the concept of rewards is found. It may be more than satisfying and sufficient to hear, "Well done good and faithful servant", but the Lord does add, "I will put you in charge of many things; enter into the joy of your master" (Matthew 25:21). It certainly would be sufficient for me to hear that "well done good and faithful servant." I would certainly hope and pray that I have pleased my Master.

Looking for the reward, however, is not so unscriptural. In Hebrews 11:25f, we are told that Moses was prepared to suffer ill-treatment with the people of God, rejecting the pleasures of Egypt, "for he was looking to the reward." The next verse tells us too that "he endured, as seeing Him who is unseen." Clearly, Moses endured in the face of hardship because he had the reward in sight, but also kept looking to God.

The author of Hebrews reinforces that point at the beginning of chapter 12, telling us to keep our eyes fixed on Jesus, but he reminds us that Jesus "endured the cross" for "the joy that was set before Him . . . and has sat down at the right hand of the throne of God."

One way of coping with hardship is to remember our final destiny. Paul in writing to the Corinthians speaks of the various battles which he faces, stating that he does not lose heart, even although physically he is deteriorating – a word of comfort for the elderly! He states that he is being renewed inwardly, and then he gives the secret of his overcoming: "For momentary, light affliction is producing for us an eternal weight of glory far above all comparison" adding that he looks at those things which are unseen (2 Corinthians 4:17, 18). He fixes his gaze on eternal matters and not temporal ones.

The trouble with us is that all too often we dwell on problems, difficulties and trials, rather than focusing on our eternal future. We do not see the time span of our problems compared with that of eternity. We certainly do not see them as "light afflictions" – we dwell on them. We may even exaggerate them. We feel sorry for ourselves. We allow ourselves to be discouraged because of our afflictions.

There was a gospel song which we used to sing in our church choir, when I was a youth, which had the lines:

It will be worth it all,
When we see Jesus:
One glimpse of His dear face
All sorrow will erase,
So bravely run the race
'Til we see Christ.

That's exactly what the apostle Paul had in mind – and Moses, and even Jesus. We will need that same attitude as we face the demanding days which lie ahead.

Yet we cannot escape the fact that Moses "was looking to the reward." In some ways that reward is seen in the fact that having fought a good fight, having finished the course, having kept the faith, as Paul said, "in future there is laid up for me the crown of righteousness, which the righteous Judge, will award to me on that day; and not only to me, but also to all who have loved His appearing" (2 Timothy 4:8). Or again, we might remind ourselves of the words of James: "Blessed is a man who perseveres under trial; for once he has been approved, he will receive the crown of life which the Lord has promised to those who love Him" (James 1:12).

The book of Revelation is full of promises for the believer who overcomes, especially within those seven letters to the churches in chapters 2 and 3. The overcomer is promised "to eat of the tree of life which is in the Paradise of God" – no mention of purgatory! We might add also that the promise to the one "who overcomes" concerns matters that every true believer is likely to receive: "to eat from the tree of life" (eternal life). Other promises include receiving a new name (i.e. a new position – compare Abram and Jacob), hidden

manna, white garments, and that our names will not be erased
from the book of life, to be a pillar in the temple of God, to
have authority over nations, and to sit down with Jesus on His
throne.

It is to those last two we must turn our attention in a
moment, but first we should note that the mark of the believer
is that he should be an overcomer. After all, it is "Christ in
you, the hope of glory" (Colossians 1:27). Can you imagine
Christ being defeated? Jesus has also given us the Holy Spirit
who is our comforter, helper or advocate. The Greek word for
"comforter" means literally "one who is called alongside". He
is there as our permanent companion unless we grieve or resist
His promptings. Paul, however, reminds us too that "we over-
whelmingly conquer through Him who loved us" whether it
is in circumstances of tribulation, distress, peril, persecution,
famine or even the sword! (See Romans 8:35–39).

To return to the promise regarding authority over nations
and sitting with Jesus on His throne. In Luke 19 there is the
parable of the pounds or minas. A nobleman calls for his ten
servants and gave them a mina each (roughly equivalent to a
hundred days' wages). The first makes another ten, the second,
five. The response of the nobleman to the first is "Well done,
good slave, because you have been faithful in a very little thing,
you are to be in authority over ten cities." The servant who has
made another five minas is made ruler over five cities. As I have
said before, we need to be careful not to force a parable too far,
but clearly this indicates that the faithful servant is rewarded.
Is the reward simply that of eternal life?

In trying to understand Scripture, we need to compare
Scripture with Scripture. The matter of sitting down with

Christ on His throne and having authority over nations seems to make it clear that ruling a city is not just metaphorical, but a reality. Let us look at this in more detail.

In Revelation 2, the promise is given to the one "who overcomes" in the Church at Thyatira. There are two groups in this church that seem to co-exist together. The first are a group of so-called believers who are involved in immorality and idolatry. They follow the teaching of a false prophetess referred to as "Jezebel". In the words of Jesus, "she leads My bond-servants astray . . ." What a serious charge! Judgement is going to fall on her and her followers. There are no promises for them for they have not only failed to overcome, but instead they have apostasised. Let those be careful who would engage in multifaith activity!

The second group are rebuked because they have tolerated this woman, though they have rejected Jezebel's teaching (Do be careful of the teaching of others). They are then told to hold fast until the Lord comes. Here again is the call to faithfulness. For those who do, who overcome and keep His deeds, the promise is given by Jesus that they will have "authority over the nations." The believer will rule "with a rod of iron" – like breaking earthenware jars! He will be given similar authority to that which Jesus received. The promise is also given that the believer will receive the Morning Star, which is, of course, Jesus; and marks the beginning of a new day, or era. That new era begins with the return to earth and the reign of the Lord Jesus.

The reference to shattering earthenware is a reminder of what God had promised to His Son in Psalm 2. The nations might be plotting against the Lord (God) and His anointed

(Jesus), rejecting their restraint on human conduct, but God has installed His King (Jesus) on His holy mountain. God consequently makes the promise to His Son: "Ask of Me, and I will surely give the nations as Your inheritance, and the very ends of the earth as Your possession. You shall break them with a rod of iron, You shall shatter them like earthenware." It is amazing, however, that in Revelation 2, Jesus should say that He is giving to the overcoming believer the same authority as He has received from the Father.

The other statement to be considered occurs in Revelation 3. It is a promise to the overcomer in the Church of Laodicea. Here is another Church with a dismal record. It thought it was so good, but it was enough to make the Head of the Church want to "spew up" which is the meaning there: "I will vomit (literally) you out of My mouth." Jesus said, in effect to that Church, "Is anyone listening to Me? If so, open up and we can have fellowship." How incredible! The Head of the Church seems to be outside it. Is that a picture of how the Church might end up prior to the return of Christ?

Yet it is to this Church that we have one of the most amazing statements. The overcoming believer would be granted to sit down on the throne of Jesus just as Jesus had sat down on His Father's throne. What a staggering prospect!

It is not just here that such a fact is anticipated. When, in Revelation 5, it speaks of the Lamb breaking the seals of the book, the song of praise arose stating that Jesus is worthy of breaking the seals for He has purchased for God men and women of every race and nation, and they are made "a kingdom and priests to our God; and they will reign upon the earth" (v. 5). The redemption of every believer by the blood of Christ is factual, so will the reign of the believers be in the future.

We might remember, however, that Paul writes to Timothy: "If we endure, we will also reign with Him; if we deny Him, He will also deny us" (2 Timothy 2:12). Scripture talks much more than we do as evangelicals – and warns – about the need to continue in faith. Again, it is the overcoming believer who will reign with Christ.

When is this to take place? Such a question raises the problem of the millennium. The Church holds three different positions on the millennium. First of all, there is postmillennialism. It holds that the Kingdom of God is now being extended throughout the world through the preaching of the Gospel resulting in a Christianised world, and that the return of Christ will occur at the close of a long period of righteousness and peace commonly called the millennium.

The second position is that of amillennialism. This view maintains that the Bible does not predict a period of a thousand years of peace and righteousness, but rather that there is a parallel development of good and evil (God's and Satan's kingdoms) until the second coming of Christ. At Christ's return, the resurrection and judgement will take place ushering in a complete and perfect Kingdom of God where there is no more sin, suffering or death.

The premillennial position often referred to as classical premillennialism is the view which was held by the early church. It maintains that with the second coming of Christ, His Kingdom in its fullness will be ushered in and Jesus will reign for a thousand years. At the end of it, Satan is briefly let loose, but then thrown into Gehenna, or the lake of fire. Likewise those who have rejected Christ will be judged and banished to Hell. Then there will be a new earth and new heaven where righteousness and peace will be firmly established.

In more recent times, however, Scofield, taking something of this view spoke of seven distinct periods or dispensations. In his dispensationalism, he believes that Israel and others will be saved during the tribulation. He also takes a pre-tribulation position (Christ returns before the tribulation) and a premillennial position (Christ returns before his reign of a thousand years).

These different views are based on whether one takes a literal or an allegorical view of Revelation 20 which speaks of Satan being bound for a thousand years during which time Christ reigns with His saints. The problem with postmillennialism is that although it sees a period of peace (but not a literal thousand years), it maintains that Satan is bound now and everything will get better and better. Yet Peter refers (in 1 Peter 5:8) to Satan going around like a roaring lion (which does not sound as if he is bound) and Paul states that "difficult times will come" in the last days (2 Timothy 3:1). Jesus also makes that abundantly clear, as we have already seen.

Amillennialism rules out entirely any such period mainly because it is only Revelation which speaks of a thousand year period, and much of the rest of the New Testament seems to suggest that as soon as Christ returns, the judgement of the unsaved will take place and a perfect Kingdom will come. The trouble with trying to interpret Scripture is that it is a little like looking through a telescope. Events appear much closer than they are. We have all seen TV pictures of motorway traffic where the vehicles look closer together than they actually are, and the distant traffic looks much closer to the foreground. If one were to read Isaiah one might get the impression that as soon as Israel was restored to the land, the Suffering Servant (the Messiah) would appear. Indeed the book ends with talking about a new earth and new heaven and yet we are still waiting for it! We all tend to simplify things a little when trying to explain a complicated concept. We do not go into all the details lest we should confuse a person. But in a more detailed explanation when the basics have been understood, then we can explain matters more fully. The Book of Revelation gives the detail to the "prophetic telescopic view".

There is no doubt that although much of Revelation is allegorical there are such clear descriptions in Revelation 20 of final events that it does seem we are dealing with actual events. Indeed, some of these ideas are found in other parts of Scripture. In any case, the early church, which was nearer to those who wrote the Scriptures under the guidance of the Holy Spirit, accepted the classical premillennial position.

We have already seen that in the letters to the seven churches, at the beginning of Revelation, the concept of reigning with Christ is made clear. It is in Revelation 20 that we see more of the detail. It speaks of those who partake in the first resurrection as reigning with Jesus for a thousand years (vv. 4 and 5). Then at the end of the thousand years Satan is released briefly from the abyss before being cast into the lake of fire (Hell). It is at the end of the millennial reign that the unbeliever is resurrected (the second resurrection), judged and sentenced to Hell.

Other passages of Scripture do seem to point in the same direction. For instance in 1 Thessalonians 4, Paul only talks about "the dead in Christ" being raised to life – nothing about unbelievers. Jesus, in John 5:29 talks about a "resurrection of life" and a "resurrection of judgement" as if they are two distinct resurrections. If that is the case, then a literal period of a thousand years (between two resurrections), as describe in Revelation 20, is not such a problem. The events described there do seem to have a counterpart in other parts of Scripture contrary to what the amillennialist suggests.

To return to the main point, however, the overcomer will reign with Christ during the millennium and for eternity, for the same note is found in Revelation 22:5 where the saints will not only have no need of sun or moon in the Heavenly Jerusalem, for God will be their light, but they will also "reign for ever and ever."

There are rewards for the faithful, and the overcomer will reign with Him, but the greatest thing is that a time is coming when the announcement will ring out from heaven that "The kingdom of the world has become the kingdom of our Lord and of His Christ; and He will reign for ever and ever" (Revelation 11:15). Daniel likewise had this revealed to him as he saw the man of lawlessness (the one who makes "alterations in times and in law") defeated, and that the sovereignty "will be given to the people of the saints of the Highest One; His kingdom will be an everlasting Kingdom, and all the dominions will serve and obey Him" (7:27). There is only one response to these things: "Come, Lord Jesus" (Revelation 22:20).

CHAPTER TWELVE

THE COMING KING

We cannot leave the matter of rewards and reigning without focusing on the King Himself. The concept of the Messiah (Christ) reigning as King is deeply embedded within the thoughts of the Old Testament to say nothing of the New. Every time we remember the birth of Jesus, we think of those words of the wise men: "Where is He who is born King of the Jews?" What made them ask such a question? Why were they told that he would be found, "in Bethlehem of Judea . . ."?

Herod was greatly troubled when he heard about the birth of Jesus, so he enquired of the chief priests and scribes where Messiah was to be born. They were able to indicate the exact town where Jesus was born because of the prophesy of Micah: "But as for you, Bethlehem Ephrathah, too little to be among the clans of Judah, from you One will go forth for Me to be ruler in Israel. His goings forth are from long ago, from the days of eternity" (Micah 5:2). It was staggering to think that Micah had given the exact location over 700 years before

Christ's birth! There is something more amazing than that which is not always recognised. Micah indicates that Messiah's birth would not be the beginning of His life, for He was "from long ago" even "from the days of eternity." In making such a statement, he is declaring the divinity of Messiah, for what child has a previous existence let alone from eternity? The Psalmist records, ". . . from everlasting to everlasting You are God" (Psalm 90:2). This "ruler in Israel" was indeed a unique person!

Isaiah also speaks of the birth of a child. Two of the names that he gives shows the same divine nature, namely "Mighty God, Eternal Father". He would also sit "on the throne of David and over his kingdom" and it would be an eternal government (see Isaiah 9:6, 7). We can imagine, just from these two prophecies, the sheer horror for Herod as he sees the threat to his throne.

Other prophets also speak of the Messianic reign. Jeremiah uses almost identical language in two passages as he speaks of "a righteous branch of David" (Jeremiah 23:5, 6 and 33:14–17). Before we proceed further, let us seek to understand this phrase.

Isaiah also mentions a shoot from the stem of Jesse in Isaiah 11. Jesse, of course, was David's father. From that same family tree would come a new shoot or branch [of the family] – a righteous person. Jeremiah declares that His name is to be called *yahweh Tzidkenu* meaning 'the Lord our righteousness'. That again is a remarkable prophecy for we see its fulfilment in what is known as 'justification by faith'. The Messiah, Jesus, would die for the sins of the world, and that, by faith, our sin would be blotted out, with God instead proclaiming us righteous. Hence Heaven becomes a certainty for us instead of us being condemned to Hell.

In Jeremiah 23, however, He also speaks of this "righteous branch" which "will reign as king . . ." and that "in His days Judah will be saved and Israel will dwell securely" (vv. 5 and 6). This is surely pointing to the millennial reign of Jesus.

Let me refer you again to Ezekiel 37 where the prophet speaks not only of a revived nation, but also of two sticks being joined together. In doing so, he shows that the Northern Kingdom of Israel and the Southern Kingdom of Judah would be one nation. Then he adds: "My servant David will be king over them, and they will all have one shepherd . . ." (37:21–26). That again clearly refers to the Messianic reign.

The most obvious references to *the Coming King* are found in Zechariah. The first mention is found in chapter 10: "Rejoice greatly, O daughter of Zion! Shout in triumph, O daughter of Jerusalem! Behold, your king is coming to you: He is just and endowed with salvation, humble, and mounted on a donkey, even on a colt, the foal of a donkey" (v. 9). It goes on to speak of a time of universal peace and a universal empire.

Unfortunately, the Jews interpreted this as Messiah setting them free having defeated the Romans. They had forgotten that prophecy also spoke of One called the Suffering Servant who would be "wounded for our transgressions and bruised for our iniquities" (Isaiah 53:5).

All the same, when Jesus entered Jerusalem riding on a donkey, they recognised the fulfilment of Scripture. They greeted Him with words from Psalm 118:26, "Blessed is the one who comes in the name of the Lord," and they added such phrases as "even the King of Israel" and "blessed is the coming kingdom of our father David," or even stated, "blessed is the King who comes in the name of the Lord" (see Mark 11:10; John 12:13 and Luke 19:38).

The prophecy of Zechariah ends by speaking of the Lord standing on the Mount of Olives and coming with his holy ones. That was exactly the message given to the disciples as they watched Jesus ascend into heaven: "This Jesus, who has been taken up from you into heaven, will come in just the same way as you have watched Him go into heaven" (Acts 1:11). He had ascended in the clouds from the Mount of Olives and He will return to earth in the same way. It then adds: "The Lord will be king over all the earth; in that day the Lord will be the only one, and His name the only one" (see Zechariah 14:4, 5 and 9).

Likewise, Psalm 2 speaks of Messiah reigning on the earth. The Psalm begins with the nations plotting vainly against the Lord and His anointed (Messiah or Christ). They seek to cast off the restraint that God would place upon them. The rulers themselves are foremost in the rejection of Christ, but God merely laughs at their futile attempts stating, ". . . as for Me, I have installed My King, upon Zion, My holy mountain." Then He addresses the Son saying, "Ask of Me, and I will surely give the nations as Your inheritance, and the very ends of the earth as Your possession." No wonder Jesus did not succumb to the temptation of Satan to worship him so that he might receive all the kingdoms of this world. God had already indicated that they were His for the asking! (I am not suggesting for one moment that Jesus might have been tempted by Satan, but rather Jesus was more than familiar with Scripture!)

The rebellion of the rulers and people would be broken as earthenware is shattered (v. 9). The Psalm ends with a word of warning to the kings of the earth to show discernment and to do homage to the Son.

It is interesting that the final rebellion is when antichrist, in alliance with ten kings, will seek to establish the kingdom of Satan on the earth. The Kingdom does not belong to the false christ and his co-rulers, but the King for Whom it is designated. It is revealed to John in his revelation that although the antichrist and the ten kings "will wage war against the Lamb", it is Jesus who will be victorious, for "He is the Lord of lords and King of kings . . ." (Revelation 18:14). Again, note the unity of Scripture, for Psalm 2 specifically warns the kings who plot against Messiah, to be wise and submit to the One Whom God has appointed as King!

The day is coming when heaven will declare, "The kingdom of the world has become the Kingdom of our Lord and of His Christ (Messiah, Anointed); and He will reign for ever and ever" (Revelation 11:15). It is worthy of note too that it is at the point when the "seventh angel sounded" referring to the seventh and last trumpet. Could that be the last trumpet when the dead in Christ rise and those who are alive are caught up to meet the Lord in the air as mentioned in 1 Corinthians 15:52 and 1 Thessalonians 4:16, 17? For me, the various Scriptures concerning the time of the Lord's return all tie in together.

The point, however, to note here is that the Lord's Kingdom is clearly established. It has already been in the hearts of the believers as they have submitted to the King, but His Kingdom will come on earth and ultimately His will will be done on earth as it is in heaven.

In the meantime, we pray, "Your Kingdom come" and "Come Lord Jesus." In the words of the hymn, we truly say:

Sing we the King who is coming to reign,
Glory to Jesus, the Lamb that was slain.
Life and salvation His empire shall bring,
Joy to the nations when Jesus is King.

In some of the difficult days that lie ahead, we will need to remember that God has uttered His decree and that He has installed His King on Mount Zion. Neither the plots of men, nor the scheme of antichrist will set aside God's ultimate purpose. Any usurping of authority will merely be temporary until that eternal Kingdom is ushered in.

CHAPTER THIRTEEN

THE NEW JERUSALEM

The Bible begins with a garden and ends with a city. While Genesis shows a man (Adam) having a personal relationship with God until disobedience marred that relationship, the book of Revelation shows a whole community in relationship with God rather than a solitary figure. The New Jerusalem is the company of the redeemed from every generation and race of mankind.

It is worth pondering the fact that in Hebrew the name Jerusalem (*yerushalayim*) means "foundation of peace". The ending of the name "*im*" is a plural ending such as is found in cherub and cherub*im*. More interestingly, however, the ending of "*ayim*" means a pair. This is seen in Hebrew words applying to a pair of bodily organs such as ears and feet. They end in "*ayim*" (e.g. *ragalayim* meaning "feet"). Therefore *yerushalayim* implies a pair of cities meaning "foundation of peace". To put it another way, the earthly Jerusalem is twinned with its heavenly counterpart.

In Psalm 122:6 we read, "Pray for the peace of Jerusalem . . ." The Hebrew for peace is *shalom* which comes from the root *shalam* meaning "to be entire, complete, whole". *Shalom* has the idea of completeness, wholeness. It is sometimes translated "well-being". Psalm 122 is saying in effect: "Pray for the wholeness, well-being, of the city which is founded on God's peace." The capital of Israel could have known that well-being and wholeness if it had walked in obedience to God's ways. Its very foundation was to be built on peace [with God].

In praying for the peace of Jerusalem, we might think of that wholeness, entirety, completion which God desires. Isaiah 62 speaks of Jerusalem's righteousness shining brightly and "her salvation like a torch that is burning" and that she is to "be a crown of beauty in the hand of the Lord." She will no longer be forsaken and desolate, but "a praise in the earth." The Church has wrongly applied this to herself, but God has not finished yet with Israel. We need to pray for the completion of Jerusalem's well-being when she truly knows the Lord, and that peace which is hers through Jesus the Messiah.

If we come to the heavenly Jerusalem, we understand clearly that its very foundation is peace with God through our Lord Jesus Christ. We cannot be a citizen of the heavenly city unless we have come into that peace which was obtained for us "by the blood of His cross" (Colossians 1:20). That is absolutely foundational. This is the foundation of the city.

While Revelation shows that city "coming down out of heaven from God" (21:10), the writer to the Hebrews speaks of us as having already "come to Mount Zion and to the city of the living God, the heavenly Jerusalem . . ." (12:22). How can that be? It is rather like the Kingdom of God. We are part of the Kingdom as a result of faith and submission to the King, but it will not be completed until the return of the Lord Jesus Christ when He will reign on the earth, and the kingdom of the world becomes "the kingdom of our Lord and of His Christ" (Revelation 11:15). In a similar way, we are a part of the heavenly Jerusalem, but its final form and completion is yet to come into being.

There is an intriguing reference to "the Jerusalem above" in Galatians 4:26. Paul contrasts it with the "present Jerusalem". He speaks of the earthly Jerusalem as being like Hagar – in bondage – along with her children. The argument in the letter is that the Jews who are insisting on circumcision and keeping the law as a means of salvation are just like Hagar in slavery. They know nothing of the freedom that the child of promise (Isaac, in contrast to Ishmael) should have known. Justification through the law is bondage, but justification by faith is freedom.

In using this allegory, he says that the true believer has come into a glorious freedom in Christ, for "the Jerusalem above is free; she is our mother" (Galatians 4:26). We can put it this way, the heavenly community, the spiritual reality has produced a people of freedom. The true foundation of peace is in Christ, who "gives birth" to real freedom: free from striving and straining to obtain salvation by our own efforts.

All through the centuries, even before Christ, there have been those who have walked by faith. Hebrews 11 is full of them! For instance, Noah in faith and obedience built the ark and "became an heir of the righteousness which is according to faith" (v. 7). Enoch, Abraham and Sarah, Moses, Rahab, Gideon, Barak, Samson, Jephthah, David and the prophets all walked by faith. They are all part of that heavenly community, a cloud of witnesses, that should inspire us today. Of course, the author of Hebrews is addressing a similar problem to Paul in writing to the Galatians. In Galatia, they were stressing the law and circumcision, but with the messianic Jews addressed in Hebrews, they were in danger of putting emphasis upon all the details of the Old Covenant rather than on faith in the finished work of the Messiah.

Much of modern Jerusalem is still in bondage not having discovered that glorious freedom in Christ. We need to ask whether the spiritual [heavenly] Jerusalem has brought life to us, or are we like the earthly Jerusalem – religious, but slaves to religious ritual and legalism in trying to earn our salvation? Come into that glorious freedom in Christ realising that we are reckoned as righteous by God through faith in Christ's completed work.

These cities are a pair, but one results in bondage through dead legalism; the other life through the peace that Christ has obtained for us by His death on the cross.

We can now look more closely at the New Jerusalem. It is interesting that in Revelation 21:9 the angel says, "Come here, I will show you the bride, the wife of the Lamb", but what John sees is the New Jerusalem. We are, of course, dealing with metaphors. In the first place the "bride" conveys the idea of two people being brought together in permanent partnership and expressing commitment to one another. Ephesians makes it abundantly clear that Christ gave His life for the Church so that He might present to Himself the Church without "spot or wrinkle" (v. 27). As we have already seen, the context there is the relationship between husband and wife where Paul compares the marriage relationship to that of Christ and the Church (v. 32). The Church has come into a place of faith in Christ, and commitment to Him as Lord. Once again, we see the importance of repentance and faith if we are to be part of the New Jerusalem. The second picture is that of the city; it consists of the redeemed community of God. The Bride of Christ is a community and not a single individual.

The description of the New Jerusalem is so graphic. First we are told that it comes down out of heaven from God. This is not some man-made edifice but, in the words of Hebrews (11:10), a "city which has foundations, whose architect and builder is God." Clearly it cannot be created by man's endeavour or by human inspiration. In contrast to Babylon (*babel*), it is a work of God "coming down" from heaven.

Man has attempted again and again to create some earthly utopia, but has failed. Communism, although emphasising a community and having all things on an equal basis, produced a totalitarian system held together by tyranny. Even the Protestant Reformers failed to produce a holy city. Planners in post-war Britain may have designed their garden cities such as Welwyn Garden City, but failed miserably to produce a perfect community. The New Jerusalem can only be a work of God – a company which has first been redeemed (set free) in Christ.

John describes the city as "having the glory of God" and being like "crystal-clear jasper" and being of "pure gold, like clear glass". Without going into too much detail, we see a city with nothing opaque in it; everything is absolutely transparent. There is nothing to hide. Adam may have hidden in the garden after he sinned, but the redeemed community of the "holy city" has nothing to hide, for our sin was dealt with by faith in Christ.

The gates to the city have the names of the twelve tribes of Israel, because it was through that chosen race that God chose to prepare for the salvation of mankind. Through them came the law which showed us our need of a Saviour. The prophets foretold His coming. Jesus Himself was a Jew. The first apostles (missionaries) were all Jewish. The Bible is a Jewish book, including the New Testament. Luke possibly is the only gentile of all the New Testament writers. In a sense, we enter the city through the revelation given by God to the Jews.

The foundation of the city, however, consists of twelve foundation stones and on them are "the names of the twelve apostles of the Lamb" (Revelation 21:14). They are "the apostles of the Lamb" not of the King, for the sacrifice of Jesus for the sins of the world is the chief message of the apostles (meaning *"sent ones"*). It is that message which is foundational for the city.

The dimensions of the city are just as symbolic. We get into all sorts of peculiar nonsense if we tried to transcribe them into metric or imperial measurements. The city is cubic in shape with the width, length and height being twelve thousand stadia. Once again we see the figure of twelve as with the gates and foundations, but this time measured in thousands. Twelve is the number of election: the twelve tribes; twelve apostles, but God has chosen thousands to be members of this community. They consists of those from every nation, tribe and language who have believed and accepted the sacrifice that Jesus made for them in dying upon the cross.

Indeed, the only ones who can enter this city are those "whose names are written in the Lamb's book of life" (21:27). This is the record of those who have put their faith in Christ and His sacrifice for sin. There is no other way to enter the Holy City. It is all of God!

John sees in the Holy City no temple like in Jerusalem, no street lighting, because "God and the Lamb" are the temple and the light. The fact is that God, the Father, and Jesus dwell among them and They give illumination. The inhabitants of that city need no other light; we never did need any other light. Jesus stated that He was the light of the world. Jesus shows us the way to the Father and the way we should go. We need no mystic or guru to guide us. There certainly will be no need for any other enlightenment in that city. God has revealed all that is necessary for life in the city.

We might continue to speak about "the tree of life" and "river of life", but simply to note again that eternal life is given by God and is not by man's efforts. It is all of grace!

The great men and women of faith have held lightly to this world knowing that they are at best aliens and strangers and pilgrims looking for a better city. In the words of the old Negro spiritual, "This world is not my home, I'm just a-passin' through", or in the words of Hebrews 13:14, "For here we do not have a lasting city, but we are seeking the city which is to come." As citizens of that city, we need to prepare for our new residence. In fact, I do not think we fully appreciate all that is in store for us, for Revelation 21 speaks of "a new heaven and a new earth" as well as the "new Jerusalem". He does indeed make all things new where there is no more mourning, crying, pain, or death. The reason why there has to be a new heaven and a new earth is because the former have been contaminated by sin: heaven by Satan's sedition, and earth by man's fall. There will be nothing to remind us of rebellion against God. All will be new. What is more, nothing unclean will enter that city.

If we are to be residents of that city, should we not even now seek to be ready?

CHAPTER FOURTEEN

THE CHALLENGE TO THE CHURCH

Many Christians are not taking seriously the issues raised within these chapters. First of all, many are looking for an end-time revival where the Church will dominate the world. That clearly will not happen! Even a cursory glance at passages such as Matthew 24, and 2 Thessalonians 2, which warn of a falling away before the return of Christ, ought to shake the Church from its composure. If I am right in saying that the Church will go through the tribulation, then again, we ought to be preparing the Church for difficult times ahead. Certainly God is going to shake all things before that unshakeable kingdom is established. We are clearly told that the man of lawlessness will be revealed before we meet with the Lord at His return. As we have seen, that means that lawlessness will be increased, resulting in many falling away. Things will get worse before the Lord returns.

We have already seen moral decadence increasing around the world. The concerns which believers have over gay rights issues is simply one area where the world is moving away from Biblical standards. As we have already seen Lot "felt his righteous soul tormented day after day by their lawless deeds", but it does go on to say that "the Lord knows how to rescue the godly from temptation . . ." (Jude 8 and 9). Yet much of the Church is living in fool's paradise because it believes that things will get better and better. We have not warned the Church of these things, nor shown that the Lord is able to support and keep us under such circumstances. The Church, however, is like Nero who fiddled while Rome burnt.

What is more, we prefer to preach on matters which entertain rather than give any depth of Christian understanding and maturity. The level of Christian preaching has deteriorated to a matter of "tickling ears" with virtually no expository preaching. People know so little of the Word these days.

We might ask where are the great preachers of former years, but perhaps the question to ask is, "Where are the great listeners?" Yet that is no excuse for poor preaching, for Timothy is told to "Preach the word; be ready in season and out of season . . . for the time will come when they will not endure sound doctrine; but wanting to have their ears tickled, they will accumulate for themselves teachers in accordance to their own desires" (2 Timothy 4:2 and 3). We might note that whether there was fruit (the meaning of "in season" or out of it), he was still to preach the word. We who are preachers must discharge our duties whether there is a response or not. "It is required of stewards that one be found trustworthy – or faithful" (1 Corinthians 4:2). We are "stewards of the mysteries of God."

We must also, as Christians, seek to be a continuing witness within the world. As the days get darker the light should shine ever brighter provided we do not water down the gospel, nor conform to the world. We can do no better than remember the words of Paul to the Church at Philippi: "Prove yourselves to be blameless and innocent, children of God above reproach in the midst of a crooked and perverse generation, among whom you appear as lights in the world, holding fast the word of life . . ." (Philippians 2:15 and 16).

Again, I do not think that the Church is equipping the saints to face the challenge of the hour as moral standards decline. Rather than being salt and light, we are increasingly conforming to the standards of the world. We adjust our position according to the attitude of the world, rather than conforming to God's Word.

What is more, there is little concept within the Church of preparing for the eternal city. We are citizens of the here-and-now, and while that may be true in part, the saints of old realised, in the words of Hebrews 13:14, that here "we do not have a lasting city, but we are seeking the city which is to come." They saw themselves as aliens and strangers within this world. We are told: "Do not love the world nor the things in the world . . . . The world is passing away . . ." (1 John 2:15–17), but we live as if this is the permanent existence rather than that of the eternal city.

What is clear is that we must get ready for what lies ahead. The future will be much more demanding upon believers than we have experienced so far in Britain. We have seen little of persecution in this country nor of opposition to our standards. That has changed dramatically within the last decade. We will soon be forced to conform to the political correctness of the day or pay the consequences.

Just before Christmas 2005, a retired Christian couple asked their local council in Lancashire whether they could display some Christian literature alongside literature dealing with the new law on civil partnerships. The council referred the matter to the police who questioned the couple for eighty minutes because of the "alleged homophobic incident".

Just prior to that an author and broadcaster on children's rights was asked on *Radio 5* whether she believed that homosexuals should be allowed to adopt (which is now allowed under the Children's Act). She replied by saying that placing boys with two homosexual men was an obvious risk. After a complaint by a member of the public (no doubt a homosexual) she was interviewed by the police because a "homophobic incident" had taken place. No further action was taken, but clearly these incidents mean that freedom of expression and thought is being suppressed by a climate of intimidation.

We feel that by the ungodly legislation that has been passed by Tony Blair's Government, and by the climate of multiculturalism and political correctness the way is already being prepared for antichrist. Changes have already been made to our laws which were once based on the laws of God. Over the second half of the twentieth century, our Christian heritage has been eroded in spite of the fact that in the Coronation Oath the Queen promised to maintain the laws of God. Unfortunately it has been her ministers and successive governments that have brought about ungodly legislation. The Church has failed to stem the tide of unrighteousness or spoken out against these things, in spite of the fact that it was the Church who required the Queen to make such an oath at her coronation. Such changes are preparing the way for the man of lawlessness.

However, the day is coming when, if we do not submit to the antichrist and his ways, we shall not be able to trade. We are fast moving in that direction. The United Nations is already controlling much, but when Satan's charismatic leader gains control, then we shall have to look to the Lord for our provision – and for His return!

At the moment the Church prefers to look through rose-coloured spectacles believing the world will get better and better. Be on the alert: a day is coming when the battle lines will be clearly drawn between light and darkness, and we had better know what side we are on! Indeed, those battle lines are already being clearly drawn. There is no place for complacency or compromise; neither is there a place for the faint-hearted nor the fearful. We are to be strong in the Lord and in the power of His might so that we might stand in the evil day. Make sure you are clothed with the armour of light!

On the other hand, let us never forget what God has in store for those who love Him. The Eternal City awaits us! Abraham was looking for that city (Hebrews 11:10). One feels that it was that very fact which inspired his life. The writer to the Hebrews also encouraged his readers by reminding them that we have no lasting city here, but "we are seeking the city which is to come" (13:14). All that spoils God's beautiful creation now will be removed, but most of all our dwelling will be with God and His Son. The splendour of that city has yet to be fully revealed, although we get glimpses of it in His Word. I believe that the glory will be far greater than we can imagine.

Brothers and sisters, remember that we are citizens of Heaven, and that when the Lord Jesus returns your body will be transformed to be like his glorious, resurrected Body. Every tear, all pain and mourning will be gone for ever in the glorious new universe. Every weakness, infirmity and deformity will be removed. All uncleanness and unrighteousness will be gone for ever. Jesus will have produced a perfect home for His bride. God, the Father will not only have reconciled His rebellious family to Himself, but will have made sure, as He says, that nothing "will hurt or destroy in all My holy mountain" (Isaiah 11:9). Our arch-enemy will never again deceive or touch the people of God. Get ready to enter your eternal destiny, child of God!

I can conclude with no better words than those of Jude: "But you, beloved, building yourselves up on your most holy faith, praying in the Holy Spirit, keep yourselves in the love of God, waiting anxiously for the mercy of our Lord Jesus Christ to eternal life" (vv. 20, 21).

Be ready for His return and all that precedes His appearing! "Even so, come Lord Jesus" (Revelation 22:20).